The Core Events of Leadership

Powerful Lessons to Build Personal and Professional Leadership Awareness

A series of leadership
event planning, publications
and training programs designed
to bring individual and
professional success!

Carlos Merla

ISBN: 1482535483
ISBN-13: 9781482535488

Future Publications

Executive Coaching–Level 300

"How to Teach, Mentor, Consult, and Coach Professionals"

Learn how to influence others through executive coaching.

Managing High-Tech Employees

"Thirteen Steps - From Techie to Tech Manager"

Learn how managers in the technology world can successfully lead!

Mixed Up

"Culture Identity, Corporate Life"

New leadership guidelines to connect culture, diversity and work-life balance!

This book is dedicated to Carlos and Edith Merla, both loving parents who became role models in teaching us all the value of family, love, and faith. My mother lived to teach children of all ages how to read and write in English and Spanish. She remains an inspiration of hope for all who knew her. Her legacy to give the gift of love remains forever in my heart.

CONTENTS

Leaders know how to follow and when to follow.

*They learn the skill of mirroring success
and then become the ones to mirror.*

INTRODUCTION AND OVERVIEW

This book is about leadership and the best practices and life lessons I learned from my professional journey of leading others. You will learn how to use seven core leadership attributes that will help you define your skills as a leader. At a bookstore, you can find thousands of books on what it takes to be a leader, but what I bring you is a fresh, real-world, hands-on approach to the core events essential for leading and winning in all that you do.

While specifically focused for those who manage or lead others, *The Core Events of Leadership* helps you understand what it takes to get to the top of your leadership game, no matter where you may currently be within your organization. Aspiring managers; tenured leaders in large, medium, or small organizations; and individual contributors—all will find that this book gives you the answers to what it takes for people to follow you and believe in you and what it takes for you to influence others. This work instructs and guides you to discover your qualities and attributes through communicating with others and gaining appropriate feedback on your leadership. Granted, there is no magic wand or secret ingredient that will bring you instant leadership charisma, but this book helps you recognize life events so that you can seize those moments and move forward to express and develop your leadership voice.

It has been written that all great leaders are also great followers. This is because they follow events that occur in their lives or the lives of others. These events should change your behaviors to help shape your leadership concepts and beliefs. Typically, an event is recognized as an important incident that can lock into your memory. It is an occurrence that can be particularly significant and is sometimes labeled as exciting or unusual. Events in our lives can be planned or unplanned; both are noted because of their significance. Finally, an event can be interpreted differently based on certain external filters such as our values and beliefs. In essence, as we experience an external event, we internalize it based on our interpretations.

This is leadership! We all may have events that demonstrate types or interpretations of leadership. Good or great, bad or ignorant, leadership is based on your experience. In *The Core Events of Leadership*, I share events of my leadership journey. Just like physicians, athletes, technicians, coaches, and other professionals and trades people do, I show you how to use "event logs" to track and develop certain changes of behavior.

Years ago, the major event in my life was when I was accepted into an executive leadership development program for the Philip Morris Companies, now called Altria Group. At the time, Philip Morris was the global conglomerate that owned Kraft General Foods, Miller Beer,

7 Up, and the big tobacco brands such as Marlboro. This executive program was a select program for up-and-coming leaders who worked in various capacities throughout the organization.

Each month for a year, fifteen of us aspiring executives were taken to remote locations to learn how the industry functioned. We were introduced to the leadership and organizational teachings of business icons such as W. Edwards Deming, who is known as the "father of modern quality control" for his work in creating the *14 Points for Management*; Peter Drucker, considered the "father of modern management," a "guru" of business thinking, writer, management consultant, and self-described "social ecologist"; Ken Blanchard, the author and management expert who brought us *The One Minute Manager* (coauthored with Spencer Johnson); and Ken Blanchard and Paul Hersey, who wrote *Situational Leadership*.

The program brought in many speakers and hosted a variety of seminars. I was mesmerized by the training and writings of Stephen Covey, who brought us *The 7 Habits of Highly Effective People*. Covey's lessons resonated with me as I was experiencing my career and individual leadership journey, specifically when learning how we can never reap the fruits of success unless we tend to the core or roots. Covey used the metaphor of the fruit tree: the roots were the source of shared vision and values, the trunk and branches were the means of communications and commitment, and the fruit was the results or profit and quality. If any part of the tree was severed, it would never produce. The mantras of his second habit, "Begin with the end in mind," and his fifth habit, "Seek first to understand, then to be understood," echoed in my mind as I internalized decisions for myself, for those who worked directly for me, and for those I counseled and aided in their careers.

Two other leadership greats who had an impact on me were Anthony Robbins, author of *Unlimited Power* and *Awaken the Giant Within*, and John C. Maxwell, who from my perspective, and that of the millions who read his book, lays down the leadership law in *The 21 Irrefutable Laws of Leadership*. He writes, "Most people overestimate the importance of events and underestimate the power of process. If I need to be inspired to take steps forward, then I'll attend an event. If I want to improve, then I'll engage in a process." His statement is spot on, and so my focus is on the process of events to help inspire you to take steps forward. To help you through your leadership process, I introduce seven core events that will help you through your leadership journey.

The core events of leadership are Significance of Acceptance, the Art of Role Modeling, Culture Identity, Confident Communicator, Five Principles (Precision, Planning, Persistence, Patience, Positivity), Leadership SWOT (Strengths, Weakness, Opportunities, Threats), and Leadership to Stewardship. There are multiple events to the journey of leadership; however, my purpose is to share these seven in the hope that they resonate with where you are today or where you want to be tomorrow. This book should help you build your confidence, recognize the different stages of leadership events, and know how best to use them to your full advantage.

As you read the chapters, you will find breaks between paragraphs that are labeled ASK. The questions will refer to the topic of discussion. Take your time to read the questions, and make a mental note of how you answered. At the end of each chapter, I have included a summary and event log section entitled "How to Lead It 2 Win It." The concept of my trademark, "Lead It 2 Win It," is to help empower you to "lead it," whatever it is, so that you can "win it," whatever it is. For this writing, "it" is about the core events of your leadership journey. The summary and event log give you a place to think through the chapter and make additional notes or answer the questions asked.

Thirty-plus years of working in the corporate environment allowed me the benefit and privilege of consulting others on how to produce the best results through a clear people strategy using leadership as the core ingredient. To further share my leadership learning, I created proprietary workshops, seminars, and coaching frameworks. Along with three independent partners, I built a consortium of coaches and a consulting practice called Merla Leadership Group (merlaleadership.com).

Our focus is to help organizations with leadership development training, provide executive coaching for tenured or up-and-coming leaders, and conduct corporate consulting to influence change and change-management concepts. As a Executive Coach and a Master Certified Coach Trainer (MCCT), I work with leaders of all levels to help develop their leadership voice and train others in the art of becoming an executive coach.

Executive coaching is an effective process when executives, at any level of an organization, recognize that they want to improve or develop a skill or are challenged in a new role or organization. Many are confronted with daily leadership challenges and need guidance, mentoring, consulting, or plain and simple hardcore coaching. As the saying goes, "If you always do what you have always done, you will always get what you always got." An executive coach is the outside observer and voice that enables you to do things differently. In my perspective, teaching leadership is the heart of executive coaching, because you cannot win until you learn how to lead.

Through your reading, I hope that you will learn how a leadership role is privileged and is measured on how you work, coach, and influence people within your organization, family, or circle of business. What you say and what you do count, and all are watching you. All are ready to follow the leader, and through these events, your leadership skills will develop you as the steward of your personal or business life.

Let's begin! Keep an open mind, have a great read, and enjoy!

EVENT 1
SIGNIFICANCE OF ACCEPTANCE

"One, who would lead others, first must be the master of self."

PHILIP MASSINGER

EVENT 1
SIGNIFICANCE OF ACCEPTANCE

This is where it all begins— with you, your surroundings, your friends, your family, the people you work with, and the peer group or team you manage. It begins with how you view and value them and, more importantly, how they view you through daily interaction and communication. How you view the world is your reality—that is, until you get feedback indicating that it's only your own perception of the world. I use to despise the conversations when people told me how their perception was my reality, because I assumed that my reality was theirs as well. In many ways it was but only as I perceived the world. It begins with understanding issues, events, and other people's perspectives through feedback and examining specific attributes. It begins by knowing the power, influence, and impact of your role models.

Significance of Acceptance stresses the importance of accepting yourself as you are as a leader at home or work, whether you are an individual contributor or you lead others. Accepting and giving feedback can be significant events, because you may be told things about your behavior you did not know or want to admit.

Many times, leaders of an organization dismiss the feedback from their peers or team or do not know how to properly react or change. Accepting and acting on feedback is what differentiates a good leader from a great leader or a manager from a leader.

I depend on my trusted advisers, mentors, coaches, and role models for feedback. When I began managing others, I was not sure how I was being perceived or accepted by the teams. As I received my first manager assessment, I was defensive about some of the feedback, but I realized that I had to change. Accepting positive feedback is easy, but accepting negative feedback is harder.

As I gained knowledge, training, and understanding about managing and leading, I began to apply my learning to real-life experience. Only then did my management feedback improve. When I learned how to use a role model for professional development, things began to turn for the best. When I used my role model as my mentor and coach, I had a trusted adviser who could guide me through some of the most troublesome challenges and issues confronting me.

Doing the Right Thing: Leadership Attributes

Years ago, when reading one of Peter Drucker's books on leadership concepts, one of his statements stood out: "Management is doing things right. Leadership is doing the right things." Drucker wrote thirty-five books on management and leadership concepts. At the time, I was managing a small organization and doing all the things a manager should do. As I grew into different management roles, my responsibility began to shift. The larger the organization I had, the further I moved from the everyday business I had to manage. I asked myself, "Am I doing the right things?"

I believe that is the question we should always ask! As you develop into roles and responsibilities, challenge yourself to reach new competency goals and develop new traits to further define yourself. If you move into a people-responsibility role, ask yourself if you are managing or leading even if you are a seasoned manager or leader.

My older brother, Eddie Merla, runs a successful Project Management Institute (PMI) practice, Duende Project Management, based in Houston, Texas (duendepm.com). In his training course, he outlines two factors of managing versus leading:

Managing consistently produces expected results.

Leading establishes direction, communicates the vision, sets the example, and motivates and inspires the team.

PMI uses some of the most influential leadership theories for its accreditation process. While some of these theories are dated, they are still major discussion points in universities, leadership classes, and PMI certification programs. Leading multimillion-dollar projects and investments through people, processes, and technology takes precision, planning and effective leadership. In my workshops, there is always a discussion of managing versus leading, and most of the participants come up with the following comparisons.

Managers	Leaders
Work within a set parameter	Work outside their parameter
Rarely focus on the competition	Challenge their competition
Accept feedback from others	Seek feedback from others
Follow the status quo	Create the status quo
Talk up the game	Inspire the game
Follow direction	Create the vision for direction
Manage the business	Lead the business

While these comparisons call out the differences between leadership and management, both are needed in the everyday practice of running a business or a project. Leadership does not change whether you run a small or large organization or if you are an individual contributor. Recognize that the larger the organization, the less you are involved in everyday management, especially if your role is to look for new business opportunities or services or to develop new technology.

The leader's role is to create an environment where people can function to their full capabilities. If you run a smaller organization, you may need to balance time for both leadership and management. The important element is to make the time to lead. When you do, it creates a significant difference in your approach to building your business to a new level.

As leadership skills become defined, certain competencies and attributes are expected to mature. A leader's maturity, sometimes referred to as "executive maturity", not to be confused with physical maturity, is about how the leader consistently presents himself or herself. There are bad, arrogant, or plain old PITA leaders in the world—PITA is the acronym for "Pain In The Ass." We have all had to deal with PITA bosses, but the focus here is the positive side of leadership, in which a leader has evolved and defined behaviors or attributes of professionalism.

I have four attributes that I view as the most significant for a leader. Granted, I could list dozens, but from my perspective, these four are critical. Most large organizations have a list of competencies to measure the effectiveness of leadership such as impact and influence, accountability, confidence, and business value. My focus is on four key attributes that contribute to a leader's ability to accept feedback as well as deliver difficult feedback

In my work in consumer retail sales and technology, there seemed to be a need for me to coach others on these traits time and time again. I recognized that there was not enough emphasis placed on these traits for the up-and-coming leaders I worked with or reported to. The four traits are courage, wisdom, value driven, and serenity.

Courage

It takes bravery and strength to do something that could be labeled risky or dangerous—in other words, it takes courage. It takes a lot of courage to think and act on your outside-the-box ideas or strategies. It takes true courage to stand up for what's right! It takes someone who is accountable and committed, someone who can support you during tough negotiations or when sales or business metrics are lagging. Courageous people know how to stand up when others are standing down.

An example of courage under fire is when I saw a district sales director in Northern California support one of her sales managers through her worst quarters. The district sales director, Linda, was my peer. Clearly, this sales manager no longer had what it took to build her sales organization and deliver the needed profit margins. Consequently, her incompetence impacted our yearly sales bonuses. Unfortunately, we were thinking selfishly with no regard as to why the sales were poor month after month.

During performance evaluation discussions, Linda stated her case in support of the sales manager and put her own reputation at risk to support her actions. She reminded us that we all went through bad sales cycles and that her sales manager, after twelve years with the company, had never before had a decline in her sales. Linda's peer group felt that if an exception was made for the sales manager, others would need the same. Although Linda needed our support for this exception, we rejected it. Our sales vice president supported the majority, and he declined Linda's request. Linda took her concern to the corporate vice president and stood up to him, informing him how as leaders we must fight for our people, especially for one who had a history of long-term results. The corporate vice president was a no-nonsense leader, and it was rare and risky to go to him on this issue, but Linda did.

Linda's courage prevailed. The corporate vice president made the exception due to how Linda presented her defense for her sales manager. Linda stressed that as an organization, we had to make exceptions for exceptional people. When the year-end results came in, we all had positive results, moving us all into the green. The sales manager exceeded her goals, and we all learned a clear lesson.

Linda provided us an example of using your courage to stand up for what you believe in. This is needed to be effective and to have a loyal following. Linda's courage was recognized in her ability to give tough messages to her direct reports and to take full ownership if she had to terminate one of her own. For her, courage was assuming accountability for the good and the not so good, and she never passed the "dirty work," as she called it, to her human resources team or other staff members.

Courage takes confidence in one's ability to do the right thing. As mentioned, when you coach clients to build their confidence, it brings out their inner courage to challenge the status quo.

Wisdom

Wisdom can be defined as the ability to know what is true or right. A person with good character, common sense, good humor, and the ability to collect knowledge is someone I classify as a leader with wisdom. Wisdom comes from experience, from working in the trenches, and from understanding what it takes to build an organization, create a technology, and lead or manage people. People say that to be an effective jazz or blues musician, you have to live the life and gather the right rhythm and feel for the music. It makes you sing from the heart, because you have been there. Good jazz and blues musicians have earned the wisdom to call themselves true artists.

This is the type of wisdom I look for in following a leader. It is the type of leadership I try to exhibit when leading and teaching others. Linda demonstrated that she had the experience and wisdom to know that her fight was worth it and was the right thing to do. Her wisdom complemented her courage to step out of the box and challenge her peers and management.

Whether it comes with experience or from within, leadership wisdom is about doing the right thing for others and for yourself. Take a look around your office, and notice which leaders people line up to consult with. They are the leaders that people tend to go to for advice! They are the ones who exhibit leadership and offer their wisdom and advice to all those who call on them. They are the ones who become your trusted advisers, because their wisdom comes from the knowledge they have picked up over the years. At times, due to reporting lines, we all must report to people who may not have all the great wisdom or intelligence in the world, but if you have the wisdom to recognize their good and bad traits, this is in itself wisdom.

Your words of wisdom come from your experiences and knowledge, and to share this wisdom is a step toward becoming a steward of leadership.

Value Driven

The most important attribute in a leader is to have core values. I mentioned how everyone lists leadership attributes differently, but 99 percent of people include "value driven" as the most important trait in a leader. "Value driven" means important and enduring beliefs or ideals shared by the members of a culture about what is good or desirable and what is not. Values exert a major influence on the behavior of an individual and serve as broad guidelines in all situations. You should never bend on your values. When you tell the world or your organization that these are the values you live and breathe by, it commits you. That's it! You don't make up interpretations or excuses if you don't live up to them. The core values of an organization are those that we honor; they form a foundation on which we perform work and conduct ourselves. It is imperative that leaders consistently "walk their talk" in representing company or departmental core beliefs.

Core values can be listed in mission statements or mantras, but they are viewed as the overarching conduct for all to follow. Core values could be the following: ethnical, dedicated, credibility, equality, friendliness, family oriented, integrity, empowerment, innovative, dependable, flexible, stewardship, accountable, compassion, and excellence.

There are hundreds of words to describe your core values, but the key is that they are the core of how you or your organization should function.

The father of values-based management is W. Edwards Deming, as presented in *The Deming Management Method* by Mary Walton. According to Deming, you must determine the core values of an organization ("system," in Deming's parlance). This allows you to determine who you should be working with—that is, the people who share your values. Once this is done, you can determine who your customers are, because you can see which people have similar values. Axiomatically, they will be interested in the product you're offering. Approaching the market in this manner allows you to focus your marketing efforts, which is essential to the success of business ventures, especially as you expand internationally.

While working at Microsoft I was introduced to Stan Slap from the Slap Company. His core program yelled that effective leadership grows out of personal values. His workshops were mandatory training for all Microsoft employees, and we recognized how our deeply held personal beliefs determined our priorities in life. They nurtured passion and commitment. Slap took the Microsoft leadership team through a journey of value alignment that connected us with our employees, customers, and ourselves. We took our teams through the same journey as we exposed our core values and beliefs to them.

In many technical organizations, the core value that comes to mind is innovation. Many high-tech leaders profess that "innovation is core to the way we do business," but when their engineering ranks hear this and start to innovate new technologies, they may be restrained. Although the company calls innovation its core value, this may not apply to everyone in the organization. For example, there may be delivery teams that focus on customer satisfaction first, and that is their core.

Core values are easily communicated using broad statements, but these like all generalizations can often prove to be inaccurate. Validate and question who you are targeting when communicating your team or company core values to ensure that they reflect the truth. The company's core values should also align with your own values. If they do not, you will struggle to succeed.

Serenity

Serenity is the ability to be humble and in control of emotions while feeling stress or pressure. It is a leadership attribute that I believe takes a lot of training and discipline, specifically when under stress to produce metrics or financials. Many leaders overreact and do not have the right patience or calmness when business results do not meet expected commitments. I have seen attitudes turn to anger as pressure builds, and the frustration is taken out on underlings. I don't know what books these leaders read that teach that "management by intimidation" still works, not that it ever did, but it shows that stress can bring out the worst in people.

Jack, a friend and one of my business mentors, was on the corporate fast track at a Fortune 500 company years ago. He had a positive reputation with the senior leadership teams, his peer group, his customer base, and most of the sales organization. Every sales and account manager wanted to hear what Jack had to say on how to move the business forward or to work with specific accounts. To many, he consistently exhibited courage and wisdom and led with his values "on his sleeve." He was a man that we thought never had a problem too tough, or had no problems at all, because he had all the right answers. He was always in control and had an easygoing way about him but never let decisions languish. He was a problem solver who operated a successful sales organization and excelled in every facet of his responsibility.

We didn't know until years later that Jack was under tremendous pressure at home. He had a son who was experiencing severe medical conditions. Each day after work or travel, he tended to his family and his son's needs in the hospital. His son's diagnosis was severe, but with the right treatment, he would live a fairly normal life.

Jack led his life and his business with such a serene approach that many of us emulated his style. Calm under pressure and in control, he demonstrated a serene approach at home and at the office. His claim for serenity was to work more proactively than reactively and to have a lot of faith in what you're doing and the people you work with.

There is a famous Christian prayer called the "Serenity Prayer" created by the theologian Reinhold Niebuhr in the late 1930s. When I talk to leaders on how to develop serenity in their organizations, many think of this prayer, which can also be found in posters or pictures. It is commonly used in twelve-step recovery programs as a reminder for strength or will power. It is a great reminder on how we should lead ourselves first so that we can lead others by the decisions we make every day.

The short version of the prayer is as follows: "God, grant me the serenity to accept the things I cannot change, the courage to change the things I can, and the wisdom to know the difference."

ASK: What are the core attributes that you look for in a leader? What are the four attributes you have?

Your definition of leadership, and the attributes that come with it, evolve through experience. As you read through the events in this book, learn to gain feedback, and develop through your role models, your leadership comfort level stabilizes. Key attributes are only part of the core needs for leadership, but choosing and defining them builds the foundation that you need to create your own professional brand in the market place. While we all create and choose our interpretations of leadership, the important element is whether or not peers, friends, family, or team members agree on how they view you.

Would they agree on your consistency of courage or display of values? When they accept your views and their feedback indicates that you "walk your talk," you will be able to answer the question, "Am I doing the right things?"

Doing the Right Thing: The Feedback Loop

This seems like an easy question. If you want to know if you are doing the right thing as a leader, ask, but the art of asking for, receiving, and delivering feedback is not so easy.

How do you feel when you're told that the way you do things has turned off your family, friends, or coworkers? How do you take feedback from those you've surrounded yourself with on a daily or weekly basis? They may give you feedback such as "We have been telling you for some time that your approach is viewed as condescending" or "I have told you a thousand times how you don't…." Perhaps you have heard "You don't take feedback very well, do you?" or this infamous line, "You never listen to me!" There is a lot of finger pointing when the feedback is "You don't listen" or "I have told you a thousand times."

When you hear these comments, defense mechanisms pop up, and you might find a way to blame others for not communicating in the "right" way. You may not mind the feedback, or you don't mind taking direction, but perhaps you don't like how the feedback or direction was presented. There is blame all the way around, indicating bad two-way communication that blocks the intent of the feedback given and the message received.

In the same context, we seem to never have problems hearing complimentary feedback. Positives are typically accepted better than negatives, and we may need positive reinforcement to help us recognize traits that we already have. Delivering and accepting negative or positive feedback has its challenges, but when you are given feedback from reliable, trustworthy sources, it's all-good. It's even better if it's positive feedback.

At twenty-one, I had trouble accepting my new position as a branch manager for Sears, Roebuck and Company. As a manager trainee for a small catalog store (or satellite store, as Sears referred to it), I was brought in as the assistant manager, working through a six-month rotation, and was trained by the store manager, Mary-Francis. She was a retired navy lieutenant who served during the Vietnam War and had been the manager of the store for eight years.

Our first "feedback session," as Mary-Francis called it, was a significant event. The week after my first rotation of working with her, she asked me to meet her in her office. As I sat on the chair in front of her desk, she pulled up a second chair and sat next to me. She said, "Look, this works differently for different people, so how do you like your feedback? Do you prefer that I threaten to fire you, or that I teach you your job so that you will improve? I can adjust my feedback approach anyway you like as long as you improve." The answer was easy and probably what Mary-Francis was accustomed to hearing. I said, "I would rather that you teach me." She said, "Okay, we will do this your way, and if that does not work, we will do our feedback sessions the other way."

This feedback session was a learning session. At that moment, my respect for my manager increased tremendously and continued to increase. Mary-Francis observed me working with some customers and informed me that I seemed intimidated by customers with a military rank. The store catered to military personal, because it was located next to Fort Sam Houston near San Antonio, Texas. She said that I was not my normal self. Customers easily noticed my coldness and change from being natural to being stiff with them. She said, "You act as if you doubt your abilities as an assistant store manager." She told me to loosen up and treat all customers the same. "Put them on equal ground. Respect them because they're our customers, but the stripes come off as soon as they walk in our doors."

It was easy for her to say, because she was more on equal ground to them than I was. I was twenty-one, inexperienced, and intimidated by the military stars and stripes that entered. However, I did not know that my intimidation had been noticed until she confronted me. She went on to say, "watch me and a few other experienced team members work with ranking clients, and learn." As I observed them, she and the team members had an easy and consistent rapport with every client. Her rhythm began with me, which was to train me, show me by example, observe how I did, give feedback on my progress, and adjust as recommended.

When my rotation was about to end, Mary-Francis had to turn in an assessment of my performance to our region director, who would pass this information to my new department head. Her report was detailed. She obtained feedback from customer survey forms and feedback from my peer group, and she supplied the director with her own feedback from working with me for six months.

The last day I worked for her, I thanked her for the time she spent with me and for the great feedback sessions. I asked her if she ever had to deliver feedback by threatening an employee's job. She replied that she had, and she told me to adjust feedback based on the situation and the person's personality. She said to choose the employee's way, which I always chose for a learning-feedback session, and that if this didn't work, to resort to the other option, "her way or the highway," meaning that the employee was out of a job. It was the first time I heard the expression "my way or the highway."

The significance of Mary-Francis's feedback loop was powerful, and I went on to use this type of feedback session for the teams that worked with me throughout my five-year tenure with Sears. Mary-Francis demonstrated how to conduct clear assessment feedback loops based on facts from my peers, customers, and observations made when working side by side with me. All this feedback helped me build myself as a manager and leader in the organization.

It was not until years later that I discovered that Mary-Francis's feedback loop followed some of the practices of W. Edwards Deming, who created an interactive, five-step method for continuous improvement in products and businesses: Observe, Plan, Do, Check, Adjust or OPDCA. Using OPDCA to give professional or personal feedback created a significant shift in my methods.

ASK: Has someone given you professional, well-thought-out, direct feedback? What approach did he or she use? How well was the feedback delivered? Have you ever been surprised by the feedback you received, whether good or bad?

Most major corporations offer in-house training on how to deliver development feedback for employees, but at times, it is a checklist of training that one has to go through as a manager. However, this type of training is better than no training. As a certified coach, I instruct clients and other coaches on this core area. I also coach first-, second-, and third-line managers and leaders on how to effectively deliver feedback based on observations or survey assessments. These are not general opinions. Executive coaches know what to look for when it comes to offering feedback that is based on the relationships built between the coach and the client; the more direct, the more value you get with your coach. This is why executive coaches are being paid, and from my perspective, when executive coaches have experience in leading others, they are the best type of coaches to receive feedback from.

Feedback on developing professional business or leadership behavior is no different from feedback in professional sports. A professional coach observes, trains, mentors, teaches, observes again, and offers feedback. Following the Deming method of OPDCA, the cycle continues until you reach expected goals. If your coach is training you incorrectly, you will perform incorrectly. "Feedback in, feedback out" is the equivalent of "trash in, trash out."

I have become a big fan of the current television show called *The Voice*. Four professional singer/performers become singing coaches for contestants who compete through the season. The coaches are well-seasoned performers such as Cee Lo Green, Christina Aguilera, Adam Levine, and Blake Shelton. Their role is to choose a contestant through a blind audition, based on voice only. When they have made their selection, their role is to coach, mentor, and develop the singers to become rising stars and win the overall competition. Their initial coaching process is to listen, observe, and give feedback. They listen, observe, and give feedback again and again until they are satisfied. The coaches even bring in guests who are professional artists to help them offer feedback and ensure consistency in the feedback given to the contestants. In this setting, time is essential, so feedback loops are quick and intense. The contestants get only thirty minutes of extra coaching from the guest coaches, and it's well worth the expert advice. During the overall coaching sessions and through the final rehearsals, the coaches are working to coach the singers to perfection. As the contestants progress through the competition, the coaching and feedback become more intense.

The show is entertaining and a great example of how those who have lived in the shoes of a professional artist work with a new generation of artists. Each contestant is offered multiple coaching and feedback sessions by experienced experts to help them become successful singers and to improve in their profession.

Open, direct feedback will mean little to the recipient if the following apply:

1. Feedback is communicated poorly.

2. Feedback is not fully trusted.

3. Feedback is given under false pretense.

4. Feedback is not acted on or is acted on incorrectly.

Let's examine these four areas and the means of feedback.

1. Feedback is communicated poorly.

I have been on the other side of the desk when a supervisor was trying to give me, as he put it, "constructive feedback." The supervisor was uncomfortable, and he took phone calls while we talked. He was not specific in his feedback.

Well-thought-out and well-communicated feedback can be effective. Feedback without clarity, facts, and sincerity can be damaging. Before offering feedback in a personal or professional setting, do your homework, get the facts, and have a clear understanding of what you want to address. Envision how you will deliver the feedback as well as the recipient's expected response. Know how to approach him or her, especially if you are addressing a sensitive behavior. When giving feedback, whatever it is, put yourself in the other person's shoes as if you were the one receiving it. This often softens your approach and adds to the effectiveness of your messaging. Customize your communication technique to get the best from your discussion. You will be of little help if you cannot effectively articulate the discussion with specific examples.

The way that Mary-Francis customized feedback by giving options is a great way to set the tone of the feedback. Poorly planned and delivered feedback is not worth the conversation and can become damaging to your relationship with a person.

2. Feedback is not fully trusted.

Because the person is your boss does not mean that the feedback can be trusted. The general assumption is that employees who view their "boss" as a "role model" should also have "respect" and "trust" for them. Unfortunately, this is not always the case, but there is nothing like getting feedback from someone you don't respect or trust. Can you imagine getting trained by or receiving feedback from a person you perceive as a hypocrite, as lacking integrity, or as unethical? Feedback should come from a trained or trusted resource. The trust I had with Mary-Francis as she guided me and gave me feedback daily was the same trust that she had established with her customers and peer group. Trust the feedback from the people who have walked in your shoes. They are typically great resources. They are the ones you see helping people with the only motive of sharing their perspective and looking out for your better interests. Trust your instincts when it comes to trusting the source of your personal or professional development feedback.

3. Feedback is given under false pretense.

At times, managers or leaders may abuse their positions by offering feedback while being uncertain of the direction they are giving. Perhaps they manipulate the feedback with the intention to not just make another person look "bad" but to make themselves appear "great." It happens more than you might think, but I have seen firsthand how leaders/ managers, friends, or family members manipulate or twist feedback. Many times, the motive for the feedback is not in your best interest. It goes back to trust. Be sure that you trust your source when receiving feedback on your development or on how to approach issues or questions. When there is doubt, rely on your other trusted advisers, and validate the feedback with them.

4. Feedback is not acted on or is acted on incorrectly.

If you have received appropriate feedback from your trusted advisers and you feel that it is given with the right intensions, it is up to you to act on it. Decide what to do next—you are now in a position to accept the feedback to work on developing behavioral traits or attributes. If you don't act on it, you may exemplify your arrogance and push aside the trust of the person who provided the feedback. Many times, rather than act on the feedback, some try to disprove the feedback by validating it with untrustworthy sources. This is ridiculous! If you received feedback from trusted advisers, there is no need to validate it with others who may be "mistrusted" advisers. They are usually a tight circle of friends or colleagues who are in the habit of agreeing with all you do, because they are friends who do not want to offend. They can be direct reports who are not always open and honest in their feedback. If you are not aware of this, denial and arrogant leadership can kick in. You will end up ignoring the feedback or acting on it incorrectly. What a waste!

Getting Feedback: Go to the Pros

In the corporate world, there are a lot of great resources to obtain appropriate feedback on your management and leadership style. As a first step in recognizing the event of Significance of Acceptance, I highly recommend that all leaders have a 360-degree feedback review of themselves. A 360-degree feedback is a system or process in which employees receive confidential, anonymous feedback from the people who work with, or for them. A good mixture people raging from eight or more fill out an anonymous online feedback form that asks questions covering a broad range of workplace competencies. The feedback forms include questions that are measured on a rating scale and also ask raters to provide written comments. The person receiving feedback also fills out a self-rating survey that includes the same survey questions that others receive in their forms.

Many companies have in-house employee feedback tools, but if there is strong interest in personal and professional development, go to the experts, and ask them to do a full assessment on you. Get the answer to the question, "Am I doing the right things?" Challenge yourself each year, each time you manage a new team, or when you have a new role, and after six months to a year, get feedback from the entire organization. If people know that their feedback is confidential, which it should be, and trust that it will be used for your personal development, you will get a large response rate.

Many trusted services and assessment experts design and administer individual and organizational assessments. There are a lot of choices and tools to work with, but the bottom line is to get the appropriate assessment done. Analyze the feedback, and work on areas to improve your leadership skills and style. Clear up any misperceptions you have built up about yourself or others, and learn how to give and receive feedback appropriately. When you get open, honest, direct feedback from a trusted adviser, personal or professional, remember that this is an event that should resonate and be remembered and acted upon. Professional feedback is essential for professional development! Challenge yourself to find out if you are consistently doing the right things.

ASK: When was the last time you had a 360-degree assessment? Have you ever? If you have, what did you do with the feedback, or what should you have done with it? Did you know who your trusted advisers were?

In *The Way to Coach Executives*, Andrew Neitlich, founder of the Center for Executive Coaching, outlines many professional, off-the-shelf assessments. I have used several of them per his recommendations:

- Profiles International: It includes Profile XT and Check Point 360, which comes with a strong assessment tool.

- Myers-Briggs Type Indicator: This is a popular assessment tool that will help you categorize and describe yourself along four orientations: how you take in information or perceive; how you make decisions and judgments; your energy orientation; and your extroverted or introverted orientation.

- Holland Psychological Assessment Resources: Holland classifies jobs into three groups: job categories, interest cluster, and work personality.

- Gallup Organization Strengths Assessment: This tool helps you identify your strengths so that you can build on them and apply them to your career.

- Professional Dyna-Metric Programs (PDP) ProScan: This survey indicates your natural personality, how you perceive how others see you, and how to adapt your natural personality to current situations.

- DISC: This is a breakdown of four primary drivers: Dominance, Influence, Steadiness, and Compliance.

I could add several more, but it is best to explore what you or your organization needs. Feedback, feedback, and more feedback fuel you with insight for continuous improvement.

How to Lead It 2 Win It®

Event 1: Significance of Acceptance

Summary and Event Log

What are the most significant attributes, behaviors, skills, or business needs for you to develop?

What things do you feel that you do right?

What areas need improvement?

Name at least three trusted advisers you can turn to, beginning with the most trustworthy. What sets each person apart from others?

If you have not had an opportunity to seek feedback from your trusted advisers or professional services, do so.

True leaders know the importance of feedback!

Recognize the power of the feedback, and take the right course of action to change.

What event happened before you sought out a feedback assessment?

EVENT 2
THE ART OF ROLE MODELING

"Leaders are more powerful role models when they learn than when they teach."

ROSABETH MOSS KANTOR

EVENT 2
THE ART OF ROLE MODELING

The final part of finding out if you are doing things right as a leader is to ask yourself if you act or behave as your role model does. Your role model is that trusted adviser who may be your mentor, coach, friend, or someone you aspire to be like. The events of finding your role models and knowing the difference between the right and wrong ones create prestige and influential changes in your behaviors.

In this section, we explore how to find or recognize role models and work at mirroring them. I guide you through a five-step process called the Mirror Map to help you develop the skill of modeling.

Finding a Role Model

A role model is typically someone we want to copy. They are people who share our values and beliefs and may already be a role model for others. Role models offer inspiration and qualities that match what we have or want to have. They are the ones we want to mirror, because we want to be like them, and they are the mentors and trusted advisers from whom we seek feedback.

All of us grow up following someone who set the example. From childhood, we use our senses to understand things the way they are, and we build in our reality of experience to assimilate what we believe is right or wrong. Think of who we first follow and emulate. Typically, it is a parent or a grandparent. It may be another family member or a teacher, a coach, a friend, a boss, a peer, a neighbor, and so on. We watch how they act, and we hear how they talk to us and others. They influence us because they are teaching us, and we learn through them directly or indirectly. These role models in our early lives use all their senses to teach us, and we learn by using our own. All information is transmitted to the brain through our five senses. We hear, touch, smell, see, and taste. What we do with this data and how we capture it is up to us as individuals.

My experience of using role modeling to develop my leadership skills started when I was a child growing up in south San Antonio, Texas. Our backyard was literally and figuratively a playground. My mother was a kindergarten teacher, and her schoolhouse was in our backyard. When she opened her schoolhouse, I went to school with her, so I started kindergarten when I was three years old. I attended school with my mother each day, so I copied how she spoke and taught the class. If she wrote on the chalkboard, I wanted to as well. If she read a book to the class, I got in front with her and copied what she was saying. Although I was a bit of a hindrance to her and the class, she accepted me playing "follow the leader," as she put it. She taught children all her life and went on to earn a master's degree in bilingual education. The way that she taught children in the classroom was the way she taught her own. She said, "Okay, kids, follow me" as she was teaching the lyrics to a song, or she said, "Do what I do" to demonstrate how to make a dance move for the yearly Christmas show. She believed in teaching by demonstration.

As I grew older and was confronted with a challenge in school, she asked, "How does your teacher tell you how to do it?" When I responded, she said, "Well then, do it that way! If it works for the teacher, it will work for you." She was clear in her message to her students and her own children: "If someone does something of significance, you can too," and "Follow success, and success will follow. Follow failure, and you will need to answer to your father." (My father handled the discipline in the family.) She knew the significance of role modeling in teaching and learning.

Recognize whatever your role model does well, and emulate it as best you can.

Role Modeling and Mirroring

Years later, I was introduced to the true art of modeling as presented by successful author and motivational guru Anthony Robbins, author of *Unlimited Power: The New Science of Personal Achievement*. He helped me realize how to use modeling for self-development. In the section "The Modeling of Human Excellence," he writes, "Successful people's lives have shown us over and over again that the quality of our lives is determined not by what happens to us, but rather by what we do, about what happens." When an event happens, what do you do to learn from it?

In the technology world, "data mirroring" is copying data from one location to another storage device in real time. The information stored in the new location is always an exact copy of the original. This is what we do when we mirror someone's behavior; we take in information from the person as we see it and interpret it. Internet "mirror sites" are used to provide multiple sources of the same information. When we go to the Internet and access Yahoo or Bing, it is a duplicate, a mirror site, but not the original.

It is the same with role modeling. When you have found a role model to mirror, it is not about making a carbon copy of someone's behavior or special abilities. Mirroring or modeling differ from mimicking, because you and your model come from different backgrounds and have different views. The difference between mirroring and modeling is one of development. At the beginning, you mirror a role model, taking only the best from the best. As you develop, perfect, and make it your own, you then model the skill. Eventually, you become the role model for someone else. You merely want to take the best of what you see and make it "your own."

In mirroring and modeling, we take the bits of what we see and put them into our personality and experiences to make them our own. Borrowing from what we see in others takes special focus and attention, especially if you are searching for specific traits to develop.

How do you choose what to mirror? Behaviors or attributes are usually acquired through many years of experience. Some "young" leaders are able to exhibit these attributes because they have gone through the process of mirroring a role model. You want to mirror the behaviors in which your role model excels. These may include courage, vocal tone, charisma, approach toward people, patience, or the ability to teach and communicate effectively.

The Art of Role Modeling is about emulating successful people. As you grow into using modeling, you develop the habits you recognized from the person you were modeling. What was once consciously difficult will become second nature as you move on to another trait that you are trying to emulate. The key is that the learning and awareness that evolve will move you into a comfort zone where limited attention on the trait is needed.

This falls in line with the four stages of acquiring any skill, and I share this with you so that you can recognize how you and others learn. The stages are from a theory developed by Noel Burch of the Gordon Training International Corporation (Burch, 1970).

The theory suggests that individuals are initially unaware of how little they know or are unconscious of their incompetence. As they recognize their incompetence, they consciously acquire a skill and consciously use that skill. Eventually, the skill can be done without consciously being thought through, and the individual is said to have "unconscious competence." The stages are as follows:

1. Unconscious incompetence. You are not fully aware of what you may have been doing incorrectly.

2. Conscious incompetence: You are fully aware of your limited capability and know you don't know how to do something.

3. Conscious competence. You are fully aware that you have mastered something and are now doing it correctly.

4. Unconscious competence. The skill or trait becomes automatic, and you do it without thinking about it.

Because you are seeking to mirror a role model, you are already fully aware of the need to develop a skill or trait. This is conscious competence. While you may not have mastered role modeling yet, you are aware that you need to develop a skill. There are many leaders who believe their leadership style is flawless and there is nothing to develop. This is where unconscious incompetence resides, and it is a harder issue to address. In role modeling, being aware of your competence, or lack of competence, of a skill you are developing increases your learning experience and ability. Effective feedback sessions should remind you of the four areas of competence.

Weighing the Good and the Bad

When mirroring your role models, you will note that they are not perfect but have perfected certain traits that you want to mirror. You may want to model all of their traits, or perhaps there are elements that do not fit your personality, so you leave those out. Examine the good and the bad, and learn from both.

An example of looking at the good is when you want to emulate those who are disciplined when studying or preparing for a presentation or meeting. You observe what allows them to be successful communicators. They may allocate time each day for preparing. They manage their calendar to ensure that they are not interrupted. They shut off their email, instant messages, and cellular phones. You recognize how they give all their time to focus on studying or preparing, and an hour before the test or meeting, they review their documents with others and share feedback to help them through the final preparations. You want to model these traits and develop, copy, and test them until you perfect them. You also recognize that there are certain things you don't like (the bad or the ugly). Your role models' preparation rituals may not be very appealing. They may develop unhealthy habits while they prepare. For example, they may drink too much coffee, not get enough sleep, and eat too much or too little. When you mirror them, sort their behaviors, and incorporate what works best for you.

I sort my reasoning by looking at the good, the bad, and the ugly when I try to perfect my speeches or presentations. I look at others who have had success in delivering presentations to the same audience and incorporate how they influenced or did not influence the audience. When I want to incorporate humor, I go to YouTube to look for stand-up comedians who best fit my personality and find ways to incorporate their style into mine. I sort out the good, the bad, and the ugly each time. It continues in every element of using role models to develop. I have never met Anthony Robbins, but I know that he has a distinct way of communicating to an audience. If I tried to mirror everything he does, I would surely fail or be criticized as a "Robbins wannabe." Remember, you want to extract only the best from each role model and make it your own by adding your personality.

You can learn what to do and what not to do by observing others you want to model. Your intuition will guide you to the right way; if not, your trusted advisers will give you the appropriate feedback. The bottom line is to think through the reasons and write them down so that you can refer to them and remain motivated to mirror your role models.

Set Your Expectations

Ensure that you have a clear vision of the expectations you have of a role model. Examine what skills you are looking to develop or what attribute or style you need to perfect. Make sure that she operates from the core values and a strong ability to inspire. Think through your needs. Perhaps you want to mirror your role model's way of collaborating with others, how she expresses her opinions, or how she get things done through others, based on her employee feedback processes. Think about the time the person gave you that "wow" effect, and look for the descriptors listed above. Think through your feedback sessions and where you are in sorting out the theories and styles. Pull out the specific attributes that you feel leaders need, and make sure that your role models have most of them. By doing this, you set the right expectations to fulfill your needs to follow, mirror, and model.

Setting up your expectations of needs is an important phase of modeling. In direct modeling, you can go straight to the source to observe or question. I knew that I wanted to model my new consulting practice on the way I was trained. When I went through my executive coaching certification program, I was impressed by Andrew Neitlich. He worked up the ranks in the corporate world until he branched out on his own and created a successful consulting practice called the Center for Executive Coaching. He developed his practice from the ground up and wrote many leadership, business, and executive coaching books, including his famous *Guerilla Marketing for a Bulletproof Career*.

By understanding the steps he took, reading his books, and continuing to be coached by him, I was inspired to model my practices on his. My expectation was to model how Andrew marketed and built his client base. I had no expectations of Andrew, although he coached me at times, but the expectations were of what I set for myself.

We all own the accountability to set our expectations of how to use a role model to develop personally or professionally. This is the same for indirect modeling. When you have little contact with the person you have decided to mirror, expectation setting is the same. The onus is on you in determining what you expect to learn from the person. As I have said before a person can mirror any person whether they have met them or not. I have never met Anthony Robbins, but during his television interviews, I hear and see his passion, and I enjoy mirroring him in my own seminars. I model his approach to bringing the audience in, and I practice my delivery based on the needs of the workshop.

I go back to what my first role model said, "Just follow the leader." There is an art to it, but it is not difficult once you develop the practice. That is exactly what it is: practice, practice, and then perfect practice.

Next, I introduce the Mirror Map to help you think through your own areas to develop. Use a thinking partner and trusted adviser to ensure that you target the right disciplines to develop. It is important to note that the art of mirroring and modeling deserves a lot more time than I am giving in this writing. There are writings from psychologists, therapists, and experts, such as Anthony Robbins, who dig deep on how to use role modeling and mirroring.

The Five-Step Mirror Map

The Five-Step Mirror Map demonstrates when and how to use role models to develop a behavioral deficit that you discovered through feedback assessments or discussions with trusted advisers. The process description is outlined below and in the following pages I have created a sample grid for you to use.

Step One: Area to Develop

Identify what you need to develop. You can review the feedback you received from your trusted adviser, your 360-degree assessment, or a personality traits assessment.

Role models display the attributes you look for in a leader: courage, wisdom, value driven, serenity, powerful, dependable, rock star, outspoken, elegant, ambitious, loyal, determined, talented, generous, funny, humble, brave, leader, communicator, cool, and influential. The person has developed a certain competency or trait, and you want to learn how to do it. If the person performed a spectacular feat, there should be a way for you to do the same.

Write down the five areas that stand out. It might be around a behavior you want to modify such as sarcasm, not being viewed as social, or being too condescending. Perhaps you display poor communication skills, or you yearn to be a more dynamic speaker or presenter. You may not be viewed as a "people person," or perhaps you come across as not having confidence or being overconfident. If you are trying to develop leadership skills, write down "leadership." If you want to build confidence or become a stronger networker or collaborator, write this down. If you want to be a better communicator, coach, singer, teacher, parent, or friend, list it.

Step Two: Reason to Develop

The reason to develop an area must be substantial enough to build the determination to mirror and grow. The feedback or assessments are there, and you have recognized that there are attributes that you need to develop, but now you must understand why you need to develop them. Your personal inner drive should give you the "why" to change, not external needs. Find the right passion, and you will find the reason to find a role model to mirror.

Here are a few of the reasons I have heard about finding a role model:

"I need to do this in order to feel more confident."

"I want to set the example and prove to myself that I am capable."

"I have been told that I need to develop this skill for years, and now is the time."

"I need to better myself so that I can grow in the organization."

"I have a story I want to tell, and I need to tell it my way."

"I know I can succeed the way he has. I just need to prove it to myself."

Substantial reasons to change focus on you first, and what the change does for others follows.

Role Models and Traits

Your named role model is someone you know, directly or indirectly, who has the skill that you want to mirror. This could be someone from your office, a celebrity, or a family member. You can list someone that you want to mirror indirectly as long as you have access to view and observe him or her as a continuous learning event.

I worked with a client who was trying to develop "executive presence," a term that is used a lot these days, specifically by managers who receive feedback from their leaders as an area to work on. Executive presence, in my perspective, is similar to leadership, because it has no one definition, but when displayed, it is easily recognized. I asked my client who he thought demonstrated executive presence, and he named the person who was his role model: the vice president of his firm. I asked him to list the top traits of the vice president and why the client felt he had the makings that labeled him as having "executive presence." Here is what he told me:

1. Consistently demonstrates confidence in communications

2. Good sense of humor

3. Street smart as well as book smart

4. Driven to succeed

5. Open to humility

As I examined the list, I asked my client if he felt that he demonstrated some or all of these traits. He said that he did, and this was confirmed by the 360-feedback he received from his peers and direct reports. He mentioned that he felt he was doing everything right and was concerned that his direct boss brought up developing "executive presence" only because he had nothing else to criticize.

I asked my client to underline the key words for each trait he listed and to place "projects" in front of each one. He rewrote his list so that it read this way:

1. Projects confident communications

2. Projects a good sense of humor

3. Projects street smart as well as book smart

4. Projects a drive to succeed

5. Projects humility

I told my client that the person who exhibits executive presence, like his vice president, is one who consistently projects traits we all have. His vice president was able to project or amplify the traits that my client possessed, so my client's homework was to practice emulating how the vice president *projected* "presence." My client was new to modeling and mirroring, but once I reminded him that he had already noticed the traits in the vice president, all he needed was to find out how the vice president projected them.

After three weeks of observing the vice president, my client began to project his "executive presence" through his confident communications, humor, intelligence, drive, and humility.

Step Three: Method

To mirror and model others, you can use different methods. Based on which role model fits your needs, the approach is either direct or indirect.

The direct method is based on one-on-one observation during a meeting or presentation, either formal or informal. This can be a dinner conversation, in class observing a teacher, or watching a professor deliver a lecture. It could be a training session or directly observing your role model as he or she interacts with their peer group. The direct method provides an opportunity to approach the person you are modeling and asking how he or she developed certain techniques. If possible, set up a meeting with the role model, and begin a direct dialogue or mentoring session.

The story of my client and his vice president was an example of the indirect method. My client did not want to go directly to the vice president and ask if he could observe him and mirror his executive presence, so he did it by watching him indirectly. The vice president held webinars and aired his press conferences on YouTube, so my client used that media to learn new speaking traits.

Direct and indirect methods require studying the habits that the role model displays. Choose the habits that fit your personality. Then mirror and model them using the same senses that your role model used to communicate with you.

Step Four: Timeline

I use this mantra when I coach people on setting goals: "If you don't know when you need to be there, you won't know if you really need to be there." Knowing when you want to develop your skills by mirroring and modeling will give you focus. The final column should have a target date for reaching your goal. By the time you reach your target date, you should be able to note differences based on your areas of development. With this target, you need milestones or timelines of specific learning events.

When you read about event five, which includes five principles (precision, planning, practice, patience, and positivity), I give a deeper perspective on the importance of going after a specific goal. Having a goal and a clear target with a specific timeline is how leaders turn into champions. This takes homework and discipline; no different than a skill you are trying to master. It is not enough to say, "I want to be like him or her," because you saw the person once or twice. It takes studying and coaching to get you there, and the discipline comes from targeting dates and tracking to focus your progress.

Event 2, the Art of Role Modeling, helps to make you into the leader you want to become. People follow leaders because leaders know how to win, and this is why we are attracted to those we call leaders. Learning how to mirror and model to become a leader is a lesson on learning how to win. One follows the other, so choose your role models carefully, and your personal and professional wins will follow.

Here is a sample of a Mirror Map, which should have specific dates and events to track your observations and direct or indirect observation opportunities.

Sample Mirror Map

Area to Develop	Reason to Develop	Role Model and Traits	Method	Timeline Milestones
Public speaking	Build on leadership, self-esteem, and confidence.	Jane Brown: Positive interpersonal skills. Elegant speaker, known to be charismatic.	Indirect: Read biographies of Michelle Obama and Lisa Nichols. Watch YouTube videos. Attend in-person meetings.	MM/YYY Biweekly
Build my network and stakeholder awareness	To expand and expose me and my team more. Gain recognition credibility.	Jack Brown: Has a huge following. People know him. He is always out there, walking around, very extroverted. Always sends communications on business updates.	Direct: Attend Jack's meetings and presentations. Meet with him to discuss skills. Shadow him.	March 1 Weekly

Your Mirror Map

Area to Develop	Reason to Develop	Role Model and Traits	Method	Timeline Milestones

How to Lead It 2 Win It®

Event 2: The Art of Role Modeling

Summary and Event Log

Which two people would you choose today as role models?

How do you measure up in comparison to your role model?

What events have occurred to you to model?

Know that the only thing stopping you from becoming who you want to be is you!

Fill out your Mirror Map and break down the areas to develop. This helps you to highlight the traits and attributes your role model demonstrates.

Role modeling takes practice, practice, and more perfect practice.

EVENT 3
CULTURE IDENTITY

"No culture can live if it attempts to be exclusive."

MAHATMA GANDHI

EVENT 3
CULTURE IDENTITY

I know you have been asked this question more than once: "What is the culture like at your office?" You might even hear someone describe your organization's culture in a way that confuses you because you would never describe it as he or she did. What is the culture like at your place of work? Can you answer with confidence that your statement would be consistent with that of your team or department?

When working with organizations and during my seminars, I find that this is the hardest question to answer. Leaders in many organizations do not have the right answer. They do not know if their culture is doing the right things or if the things they are doing are right for their culture.

This disconnect is common. High-ranking leaders of large organizations are quick to answer with pride. However, when you go down a rank or two and then to the first-line teams that work directly with customers, partners, or developers and engineers in the technology world, you get totally different answers. When I tell the CEOs or vice presidents of the inconsistent answers, they say that they need to do a better job of communicating what their culture is in their department or business.

Granted, there are a lot of great organizations that have clear and consistent cultures, but for the most part, I find culture identity issues. As the organization increases in size, so does its gap of culture understanding.

Through the event of Culture Identity, you learn the four components of culture awareness:

1. Culture insight

2. Connecting cultures

3. Culture diversity

4. Creating a ROOTS-based culture (Recognition, Observance, Optimism, Trust, Stewardship)

Culture Insight

The term "culture" was first used in this way by the pioneering anthropologist Edward B. Tylor in *Primitive Culture,* published in 1871. Tylor said that culture is "a complex whole which includes knowledge, belief, art, law, morals, custom, and any other capabilities and habits acquired by man as a member of society." Of course, it is not limited to men. Since Tylor's time, the concept of culture has become the central focus of anthropology and studies of human development.

Tylor outlined three critical areas of cultures.

Traditional cultures. This is the body of culture traditions that distinguish your specific society. Those who share your culture do so because they acquired it. Traditional cultures share the same language, faith, geography, and family culture.

Sub cultures. These are seen as being part of the cultural mainstream of the nation. In complex, diverse societies in which people came from different parts of the world, they often retain many of their original cultural traditions. Subcultures have shared traits, ethnicities, identities, or ancestral backgrounds. In the US, it is common to label someone as "German American" or "Italian American," etc. This is a subculture, removed from its traditional culture.

Universal cultures. No matter where people live, they share universal features, divisions, categories such as age, gender, relations status, labor division, and leadership roles. Universal cultures are learned behavioral patterns that are shared collectively by all of humanity.

From these cultures, the inevitable arises: the development of a working or organizational culture. All three cultures have a major area of commonality, which is that the people have created habits around how they live, communicate, and produce to create their community, including the traditional foods that their culture produces. They are accustomed to their language culture, which can be a mix of verbal or nonverbal communication. They have created a cultural habit of family unity, religion, and respect for elders in the community. These cultures are the way they are because they worked and adapted to their environment, surviving generation after generation. You have a working adaptive culture that continues to produce and develop in a viral way that spreads through geographies.

Understanding this should help prevent a breakdown when diverse cultures come together. In a working environment, the differences are typically in the areas of language or food. The traditional cultures are unique from others but not enough to be detrimental to achieving success. Subcultures are a subset of the traditional; however, some may adapt to local cultures faster while still maintaining their core beliefs, traditions, or religion. Hinduism, Islam, Judaism, Mormonism, Christianity, and many others are examples of religious cultures that have adapted to geographies. With universal cultures, the same beliefs or morals apply wherever the cultures land. Labor and leadership divisions remain the same throughout the world; however, in some cultures, such as Asian culture, leadership ranks in the corporate world are strictly enforced and can be viewed as militaristic.

Connecting Cultures

While working at Microsoft, all you have to do is to walk into the campus cafeteria to recognize the diversity of cultures. Like many international high-tech companies, Microsoft caters to the cultures of employees with a variety of foods: Korean in one corner and Mexican in another, along with Indian cuisine and good old-fashioned American hamburgers. Food remains a great connection to culture, but within the working teams or the organization are hundreds of interpretations of the culture and subculture environment.

When working with clients, I asked about the working culture in their company and department. I heard first-, second-, third-, and fourth-line leaders give their interpretations. All were passionate when they explained their working culture, yet the descriptions were based on their own interpretations.

I explored further and went to the front-line sales, developers, and technical support teams to find what they had to say. Interestingly, most were also passionate about how they viewed the working culture, using terms like "customer focused," "diverse," or "easygoing." In the US South, it is typical for organizations to claim that they have a "get 'er done" attitude, meaning a hard-working culture that gets the job done no matter what. My main takeaway was that describing culture was like describing a football or hockey club. In many cases, there was a lot of camaraderie and great morale when things were going well. When there was a positive connotation behind the description of the organization's culture, nomenclature was of little significance.

I recently surveyed an organization and asked the employees what their work or organization culture was like. The picture below illustrates the responses. The triangles labeled with an X represent employees who did not know what their culture was. The triangles with a Y represent employees who took a guess but were unsure, and those with a Z represent employees who did not care. The other labels such as "value based" or "customer focused" were given quickly and based on the current working environment. Cultures that merge to create one organizational culture or subculture can be convoluted.

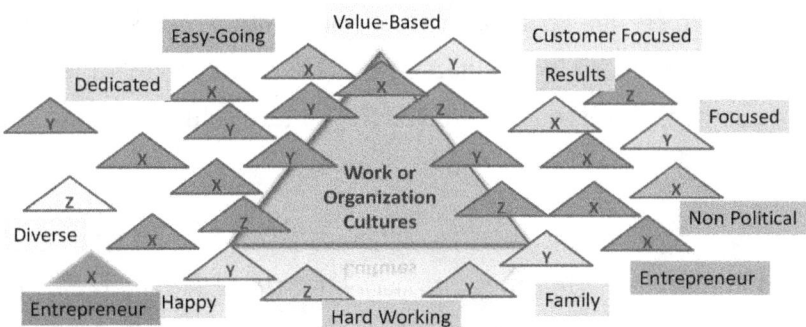

When morale or business results were not up to expectations, the tone of the culture description was low and at times negative. The significant difference between a highly motivated or "connected" culture environment and one that was more negative and disconnected always pointed to the leadership of the organization. The leader held the responsibility for the culture's esprit de corps.

A well-known leadership icon at Microsoft was a services director named Aaron. He had been with Microsoft for more than twenty years. Through coming up the ranks, holding a variety of positions, and running multiple organizations, he had a reputation of running a sharp, deep technical team of engineers that always had high customer satisfaction ratings, low turnover, and the highest internal organization health index (an employee satisfaction rating). His was a "people-first culture." Everyone who knew Aaron and the people on his team recognized what that meant. Aaron put his team—his people—first, and he expected his managers to do the same. He was the first to walk the halls in the morning to see how the team was doing. At events or meetings, he was the "greeter" at the door who welcomed all in. He worked to ensure that they had the right hardware and up-to-date tools so that they could be proficient with their customers. If people called in sick, he checked on them at home and offered additional time off if they needed it. By his "people first" actions, Aaron "walked the talk" of creating a collaborative connecting culture that benefited the teams and the clients they served. He created the culture, and the organization followed.

ASK: Who sets the tone for your work culture? How would your department or team describe your work/office culture?

To connect with the strategies of a business, it is clearly the leader who sets the tone for the cultures to connect. It is impressive how some cultures stand the test of time and some wither as they change but their core remains. Daryl R. Conner, author *of Leading at the Edge of Chaos*, describes how three organizational variables—leadership, context, and culture—should be in place and supportive of each other. Conner explains that leadership and executive behavior will guide the organization most effectively in changing circumstance if they are predisposed toward opportunities inside and outside the organization. Context (vision, mission, and strategy) is needed to succeed in unstable market conditions. The context set by leaders needs to articulate and embody the characteristics of resilience. Culture beliefs, behaviors, and assumptions displayed by the organization's associates must reinforce the characteristics of resilience. This remains especially true in the changing landscape of diversity and global business expansion.

As a leader in an organization, you must make cultures work, not collide. It is up to you to embrace traditional cultures, subcultures, and universal cultures and know how to use them as beneficial assets to shape the culture in your organization for the better. These cultures – traditional, sub, and universal – thrive in any geographical location because a person's culture is embedded in them; people believe in the traditions they have worshipped and lived. Professional and organizational cultures can become as strong and valued as personal cultures when the leadership allows them to thrive.

Diversity of Cultures

Understanding the aspects of personal culture and professional organizational culture is a clear demonstration of how diversity interrelates. Diversity in the workplace is not just about respect for race, ethnicity, or religion. We cannot have a clear understanding of culture, personal or professional, without bringing to light the importance of diversity.

Diversity means a variety of something such as opinion, color, or style. It is about inclusiveness and socioeconomic and gender variety within a group, society, or institution. In every organization, department, or team, diverse opinions, beliefs, and cultures develop. It can be an existing culture that has served the organization over time or a changing culture that varies by department. You can have a "global culture" within an organization that is redefined to a smaller culture or department. It is important to allow diverse opinions and options within your culture but still maintain an overall culture that best defines the entire organization.

There is no forcing organizational culture, just as there is no forcing personal culture. We cannot discriminate personal culture based on race or nationality, nor should we discriminate on professional culture. They develop over time and become ingrained into how we live at home or at work. As a leader, you can create the vision of the type of culture you want in your organization.

I became friends with a young Chinese engineer named Benny Chong. He was originally from Kowloon, Hong Kong, and when he moved to Texas to join Microsoft, he had been in the US for fewer than three months. Benny was a decent young man who was well educated and trying to make it in the US. He was also the first of his generation to live outside of Hong Kong. He wired money to his parents each month, and he kept to himself most of the time. These behaviors led everyone around him to characterize him as a private, introverted person.

When he joined Microsoft, his boss (who was not very knowledgeable on diversity) introduced Benny as "the new technical engineer from

Korea." When I saw Benny at our campus cafeteria eating alone at a booth, I joined him, and we began talking. I let him know that I had never been to South Korea but had a strong interest in visiting Seoul. With his strong accent, Benny conveyed that he was not from Korea but from Hong Kong. He said that he corrected his boss during a one-on-one meeting, but his boss continued to forget. Benny told me how it was not proper for him to remind or correct his superiors. I was embarrassed for his boss, and for us as a company, for not defending Benny's origin and introducing Benny by his nationality as the leading point of who he was. The introduction could have simply been to share Benny's technical knowledge.

Benny and I had a great conversation regarding the cultural differences between Americans and Chinese, and I learned much about Kowloon, Hong Kong. He told me how he was struggling to assimilate within the Microsoft culture and within the team, especially because his manager kept introducing him as Korean. At the end of our lunch, Benny agreed to place a sign on the outside of his work cubicle that read, "Hi, my name is Benny, and I am new to Microsoft. I am a subject matter expert on SQL Server and Internet Explorer. I have just moved here from Hong Kong, and I enjoy playing soccer and table tennis!"

All who passed Benny's cubicle read the sign, which led to conversations regarding his areas of interest. People knew about his technical expertise but not his athleticism in soccer or his passion and skill at table tennis. Most importantly, they learned that he was not Korean but Chinese. His manager took notice as well, but unfortunately, he simply said, "Oh, I thought you were from Korea." I would have thought that Benny's manager would have taken more interest in correcting his mistake, because he once confided in me that he felt he was being stereotyped because of his looks and last name. Bennie's boss was from Peru and was often mistaken as Mexican. This was primarily due to the high number of Mexican Americans who lived in Dallas. The issue that bothered the boss was the same one he put on Benny. For Benny, the fact that his manager acknowledged his Chinese background was fine. The poster created a network for Benny that led him to join a company-sponsored soccer team, and within a few months, he took second place in the table tennis contest held in the company cafeteria. He lost to a Korean American.

Knowing where people come from builds the diversity of knowledge and strength in the workforce. Knowledge sharing from this aspect is the key to success. If you hire from a partner, be prepared to learn the best practices of its culture. When you hire from your competitors, embrace and respect their cultures, and find out all you can about them. Compare your working culture to those of your competitors and customers, and look for opportunities to improve.

I know of a senior vice president from a Fortune 500 company who told his two thousand-plus employees to recruit and hire people throughout the industry! He said, "Once you hire them, remind them that they are now with the best company in the industry. Have them forget what they think they know, and teach them our corporate way to success." This was a misstatement, because the company was losing market share at the time, and the best advice to give his management team should have been to recruit and hire from within *and* outside the industry and learn from the successes and cultures of others. Culture diversity at its best is knowing that your own culture is not the only one that may bring you success.

A leader's acceptance of culture diversity tells the organization that you are doing the right things and expect others to do the same. Inspect what you respect! While you may practice and lead your organization with the integrity of diversity, you should gain feedback from your organization to ensure that all have opportunities to embrace their culture.

Building a ROOTS-Based Culture

Researching and becoming further involved with cultural issues in the workplace allowed me to understand my experiences and where my culture comfort zone was. I have seen the power that complementary cultures have in developing winning teams or in derailing an organization—focusing on gossip, finger-pointing, and bickering about how things should be rather than getting things done. I have seen how organizations fail to accept the diversity of personal cultures and do not use them to their full advantage.

Taking these into consideration, I created a ROOTS (Recognition, Observance, Optimism, Trust, and Stewardship) Based Leadership model. This concept focuses on the front-line of an organization's culture. It is used as the foundation of bottom-up leadership which considers the opinions of lowest levels of the organization and combines the insight of a "clan and adaptable culture" framework.

The concept of "clan culture" comes from research conducted by Kim Cameron and Robert Quinn, who wrote on organizational effectiveness and success. It is based on the Competing Values Framework (CVF), which is a great tool for thought leadership. It focuses on how various aspects of organizations function in simultaneous harmony and tension with one another.

CVF produces polarities like flexibility versus stability and internal versus external focus, and these polarities were found to be most important in defining organizational success. Cameron and Quinn used the polarities to construct a quadrant of cultures:

1. Adhocracy culture (external focus and flexible): A dynamic workplace with leaders who stimulate innovation. In this view, cultures are creative and innovative.

2. Market culture (external focus and controlled): A competitive workplace with leaders who act like hard drivers. It primarily focuses on the value to the customer. Market-driven cultures are typically competitive and aggressive.

3. Hierarchy culture (internal focus and controlled): A structured and formalized workplace where leaders act like coordinators. It values control, efficiency, and predictability.

4. Clan culture (internal focus and flexible): A friendly workplace where leaders act like father figures. This culture is collaborative and driven by values such as commitment, communication, and individual development. Motivation results from human development, employee engagement, and a high degree of open communication.

Clan cultures are strongly associated with positive employee attitudes and product and service quality, whereas market cultures are most strongly related with innovation and financial effectiveness.

When I looked deeply into the CVF model to understand these cultures, I was attracted to the research done on clan cultures. I was a leader who worked in multiple organizations. As a consultant receiving feedback assessments from every level, I noticed that clan culture environments emphasized the real workings of the organization. The focus was on how flexible the cultures could be. There was little concern about the rules and more focus on the vision of success, primarily on outputs and outcomes. The organizations worked more effectively given autonomy and succeeded when allowed to operate as a family with shared goals driven by loyalty to one another. As a leader creating a clan culture environment, the role was more of a facilitator who gives support and encouragement to succeed.

The idea of an "adaptable culture" comes from John P. Kotter and James L. Heskett (*Corporate Culture and Performance*), who describe how three primary cultures exist within an organization: strong, strategically appropriate, and adaptive. Each has been identified with high-performing organizations and has particular implications about motivation in the workplace.

A strong culture is the most widely reported, because it is based on results from high performance. The reasons for this are goal alignment, motivation, and the resulting structure provided.

A strategically appropriate culture motivates due to the direct support for performance in the market and industry. "The better the fit, the better the performance; the poorer the fit, the poorer the performance." (Kotter, Heskett, 1992)

Adaptable cultures allow an organization to perform at a high level over a long period of time. It must be able to adapt to changes in the environment. There is a shared feeling of confidence: the members believe, without a doubt, that they can effectively manage whatever problems and opportunities come their way.

When I led a sales division for consumer goods, we had developed a strong and adaptive culture that was strategically aligned with our sales goals. When competition aggressively approached our customer base, we adapted to new strategies to combat competitive encroachment. Adaptability in our selling culture created a readiness for winning strategies. Adaptability in organizational cultures is much like the adaptability of traditional and subcultures that are resilient due to their adaptation to the environment.

As demonstrated by the figure below, creating a clan and adaptive culture stems from the core front-line of the organization. The front-line, fueled with organizational ROOTS, creates a bottom-up leadership culture. This is a ROOTS-based culture, and if the front-line is ignored, the culture is lost. When acknowledged and used as a listening system to produce new strategies, or change results, the front-line organizations are able to high performance.

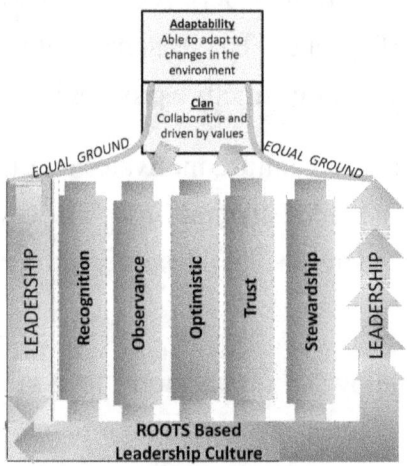

ROOTS-Based Leadership Defined

A ROOTS-based culture allows the front-line teams to give the input needed for immediate feedback to the senior leadership teams on what is working and what is not. In the clan culture model, a significant amount of collaboration is put into the customers' needs and what the organization needs to succeed. Through the adaptive cultural approach, the organization can easily adapt to meet market or customer demands.

Senior leadership teams must put front-line teams on equal ground and allow the culture to develop with their guidance and nurturing.

ROOTS-Based Leadership is about the core organization and the leadership and culture that live within. It focuses on the customer-facing teams as a service that fuels the results and profits. For the organization to become more profitable, leadership must be collaborative, so the flow of communication should be a two-way stream. This flow is based on how well the roots are positioned within the organization and how the leadership teams embrace and respect the value of the front-line teams that work with customers on a daily basis.

While doing extensive work with mergers and acquisitions teams, I was chartered to bring in newly acquired organizations to the Microsoft culture. As expected, the integration was challenging, as I was responsible for combining one technical organizational culture with another. One of the CEOs I worked with said, "It's like bringing two tribes together to make one; there are going to be a lot of tribal meetings to determine whose ways are better." When you dig into the existing culture of an acquired business and understand how it works and what led to its success, many times it is clear that its way of doing things is better than your own.

Taking the time to learn how things were done, by working inside the core roots of the organization, always benefitted and made the integration and incubation periods more seamless. The key to onboarding organizations was to recognize their culture value, observe the net worth they brought to the business, and share their optimism of how they viewed the significance of their daily roles. Employing the same trust that customers put in them demonstrated culture understanding. The front-line teams are the stewards that drive the culture of the business. As a leader for the stewards, you set the tone for the culture to be recognized, observed, optimistic, and trusted.

Recognition

I sometimes use the term "recognized value," which ensures that leaders consistently give recognition to the heart of an organization that is the front-line. They recognize not just what they do but how they do it, how they represent a product or service, and how they communicate, sell, and represent the business and the company or department. Recognition promotes the ego, but recognizing the value of all those who come in contact with the customers daily, directly or indirectly, is powerful.

Public Recognition. There is nothing more rewarding than for an individual contributor or team to be publicly recognized for their work and accomplishments. Public recognition can be executed via internal communications shared with peers and up through the management chain. It can be external communications posted on websites or in publications such as newspapers and trade magazines.

Private Recognition. Just as important as public recognition, but at times more impactful, is for individuals to be recognized during a one-on-one conversation with a superior. Private recognition creates an intimacy and an understanding of self-worth. A leader who promotes a winning culture and takes the time to privately recognize individual value is making a powerful statement that will spread throughout the organization.

Listen to and recognize the voice of the customer through your front-line organization. Expressing sincere appreciation and acknowledging them by saying thank you for all they do brings more value than a leader may expect.

In event seven, Leadership to Stewardship, I describe how important it is to give recognition to the the organization that has direct contact to the customers. Recognition for the work the front-line does every day allows stewardship concepts to thrive.

Observance

As my first professional mentor, Mary Francis, said, "One cannot recognize what one has not observed." For the leader of an organization, observance is twofold. If you expect certain behaviors of others or specifically of your organization, they must have the opportunity to observe you. Once you have taught or demonstrated a behavior, it is time to observe *them*.

It goes back to the Deming method for continuous improvement, OPDCA. Using OPDCA to give professional or personal feedback is also a way to measure performance, to observe and/or be observed. Plan, do, check, observe again, and adjust as needed.

Another anecdote that applies to observance is MBWA or "Management By Walking Around." Leaders or team managers cannot observe anything from behind their desk or from the "ivory tower" of their headquarters office. You cannot get the pulse of the culture unless you are out there to feel it and touch it. It allows the teams to see you engaged in understanding the day-in, day-out needs of the business.

In the US, there is a reality TV show called *Undercover Boss*. A CEO goes undercover, posing as a front-line manager, sales clerk, or technician, to find out the real issues occurring in the organization. The CEO typically finds hard issues that had not been addressed or had not made it up the chain of command. Realistically, if all things are working within the organization, there should be no need to go "undercover."

Leaders at every level should carve out the time to understand business issues by rolling up their sleeves, going into the field, and observing, planning, doing, checking, and adjusting as needed.

I have worked with technical support teams that went to customer sites to conduct technical workshops or proactive or reactive break-fix services. A majority of these engineers stated that their direct manager had never been with them on a customer site. Their manager had never seen them interact with customers while conducting a technical seminar. Their manager was still responsible for evaluating their overall performance, which was typically based only on customer satisfaction surveys and had nothing to do with one-on-one interaction and observance.

"You can expect what you inspect," Deming says. If you do not take the time to inspect or observe, you will never understand the nature of the culture within.

Optimism

Optimism in an organization is the propensity to consistently look at the bright side of any situation and expect the best possible outcome from any series of events. Ambiguity from constantly changing organizational events is inevitable unless optimism remains in the forefront. When you fuel the organization with optimism, the culture environment will reciprocate. Optimism is powerfully motivational and is one of the cornerstones of successful organizational cultures.

Susan Heathfield is a human resources expert. In her article "The Power of Optimistic Thinking" on About.com, she wrote, "The power of optimism cannot be overrated as a factor in success and personal growth and development. Optimism allows you to see the positive aspects of any situation and enables you to capitalize on each possibility.

Optimism may be partly responsible for success in most aspects of life. Some research exists that demonstrates that optimism results in higher achievement." (Heathfield, 2009) Her insight has resonated with me and proved beneficial when working with others and setting my personal goals. Having an optimistic viewpoint, setting goals, and working toward those goals keeps us motivated to succeed.

The two primary elements that keep an organization filled with optimism are communication and inclusiveness! As an example, when I worked with a technical division during its first internal merger into the larger Microsoft division, the one hundred-plus employees were full of ambivalence. Resistant to the change and skeptical of their new leadership teams, the front-line team members started requesting transfers. It was as if the entire team looked into a crystal ball and predicted termination during the first week of integration. This was not the case, but as soon as the merger was announced, a flood of transfer requests came in. The leadership team reacted by placing a moratorium on transfers, which increased the overall ambivalence.

Unintentionally, our leadership team created pessimism within the organization and disrupted a culture that was labeled as collaborative and family oriented. I was a part of the leadership team and in hindsight, rather than making an announcement and then working through the change, we should have included key team members in our strategy discussions. We needed to involve them and understand their issues from the bottom up and outline the benefits for the integration of teams. Our leadership team had an optimistic vision of the integration, but in the process, we created pessimism throughout the ranks. As we debriefed on our key learning, we incorporated a more collaborative and inclusive strategy for our integration processes. Optimism results in higher achievement and inclusiveness.

Trust

There is not a lot of news when it comes to organizational trust. If you don't trust your managers or front-line, shame on you! When I hear a leader say, "I don't trust the judgment of my front-line" or "I don't trust my manager's feedback," I hear an accountability issue that has not been addressed. The managers are not addressing the trust issue. If you don't trust them, why are they there? If you have lost trust, ask why. In any relationship, trust is core to building an organization. As a leader, you must be able to trust what the organization is saying or needing. On the other hand, it may be the organization or the front-line that does not trust you or the larger organization. Perhaps you or your department heads have committed to resources or additional headcount or sales incentives that they did not provide. The front-line lost trust in its team or organization. The results easily impact the bottom line. Employee turnover may occur, and morale may be lowered.

Trust is the foundation of leadership. Leaders often forget how the core value of trust can be a game changer in their organization. I have seen my share of leaders who abuse their trust by manipulating others. Success inhibitors to building trust, sometimes called "derailers," contribute to leadership failures. Common success inhibitors to building trust were identified through open discussions with many of the front-line teams I worked with. They provided examples from their experiences of working with a variety of managers and leaders. Not all leaders demonstrate these trust inhibitors, and they may not appear until late in an individual's career, but identifying them should help to prevent them from happening.

In *The Five Dysfunctions of a Team*, Patrick Lencioni breaks down the differences between teams that exhibit trust and those that do not.

Teams with an absence of trust

- Conceal their weakness and mistakes from one another

- Hesitate to ask for help or feedback

- Hesitate to offer help outside their areas of responsibility

- Fail to recognize and tap into another's skills and aptitudes

- Hold grudges

- Dread meetings and find reasons to avoid spending time together

Trusting teams

- Admit weakness and mistakes

- Ask for help

- Accept questions and input about their areas of responsibility

- Give one another the benefit of the doubt

- Take risks in offering feedback and assistance

- Focus time and energy on important issues, not politics or posturing

Other trust inhibitors may include the following:

1) Failure to stick to commitments

2) Lacks passion for the business

3) Talks more about others and spreads rumors

4) Shuts down or shuts out others

5) Uses the term "trust me" after a person has already lost credibility

6) Does not "walk the talk"

7) Unable to make up his or her mind and delegates decisions

8) Consistently makes wrong decisions on choosing new staff/ managers

9) Not open to feedback

10) Lacks respect and credibility from peers and team

Trust remains the foundation for any relationship, including the trust that people place in their peers, staff, and leadership teams.

Stewardship

The road from leadership to stewardship is detailed in event seven, but as a core component of a ROOTS-Based Culture, it is about accepting the accountability and the knowledge transfer of leadership success. What led you or your team or department to have significant success with your customers must be shared. Stewardship is the open and honest commitment to team success, not individual success. Share the feedback, share the learning, share the pain, and share the best practices learned from the experiences, good or bad. Stewards of your business will be easily exposed when the environment welcomes diversity in cultures and in thought. As the saying goes, "What got you here today may not be enough to get you there tomorrow." Stewardship builds resiliency, and the front-line organization is the real steward of your business.

A ROOTS-Based Leadership culture is an event that puts the organization on the same playing field, which means that all are focused on results, profits, sales, or customer satisfaction. Bring in the right level of recognition, organizational culture, and resource understanding. Conduct a trust check, and get on board to the road of stewardship by putting all on equal ground!

Putting All on Equal Ground

No matter the position in a small, medium, or large organization, know that we are all on equal ground. An organizational culture that recognizes the value of its resources at every level is destined to succeed.

Organizations will even succeed when challenged with figuring out how to survive a wave of initiatives that stretch them and their teams. When organizations are placed on equal ground, it creates a shared thinking on how best to beat the competition for market share. All will have share the same "risk." W inning in the marketplace is not just the responsibility of a manager or the wish of the corporation, because when you work on equal ground, you have the same concerns. If the corporation or the boss is winning, you all win! If the front-line individual contributor who works daily with customers, supporting their needs, is satisfied with his or her working culture, customers will recognize the difference. If there is success in the business world where you are employed, there is success in your personal world.

You may hear companies state that their culture is "people first" or that "employees are our number one priority." While there are many who stand by this, many demonstrate it only part of the time, and many are not there yet. They may mean well, but the front-lines to them are the lower-level sales teams or engineers who, in management's mind, don't understand the bigger picture of the product or service. A disconnect continues when the roots become separated from the sources of information, vision, mission, and a full understanding of the customer's needs.

As shown in the diagram, the ROOTS-Based Leadership model recognizes the importance of equal ground and how it brings a consistent flow of communication from the front-lines to the top of the organization chain and vice versa. However, management does not hear the voices of the customer and the front-line support engineers and consultants. I know of many general managers and vice presidents who manage more than fifteen hundred front-line employees but rarely conduct face-to-face meetings with their teams. They rely on information from their first- or second-line management staffs, leaving a huge disconnect between the needs of the staff, customers, and the corporation.

From a ROOTS-Based Leadership view, it is always customers first; the organization follows and influences the rest. While the chain of command has its importance, it can sever the flow of free, open communication. The pulse of the customers and front-line needs is lost.

Overall, leaders manage the event of Culture Identity. Create an environment where culture diversity, recognition, and team collaboration work. Use this learning to rethink your strategy, and focus on creating a cultural awareness session to find out the needs of the organization on all levels.

How to Lead It 2 Win It®

Event 3: Culture Identity

Summary and Event Log

Understanding your work culture, and creating an environment or listening system to ensure that the voice of the organizational culture is heard, can make or break companies. Focus, listen, and bring in a ROOTS-Based Leadership culture.

Use this learning to rethink your culture strategy and create a culture-awareness session with your organization.

Ask yourself what your work culture is or what you think it should be.

Ask your organization's people what they think their work culture is like.

What event has happened to you when you were defining or assimilating your own culture? What were the challenges or differences?

Do you take your culture with you wherever you go? If not, why?

Who is responsible for driving the culture in your organization?

List your vision of a culture, and get feedback from your team.

EVENT 4
CONFIDENT COMMUNICATOR

"There can be no friendship without confidence and no confidence without integrity."

Samuel Johnson

EVENT 4
CONFIDENT COMMUNICATOR

Through the events of Significance of Acceptance, the Art of Role Modeling, and Culture Identity, you probably recognized several aspects of how you view yourself and your environment. Now it is time to think through how you balance your level of confidence and how you exhibit leadership attributes. As with most events that occur in your life, personally and professionally, you need to display a controlled and balanced leadership style. Self-confidence, overconfidence, or low confidence can become game changers for leaders, and the most common mistake they make is to take their leadership role for granted. They do not recognize how effective communication is the key to demonstrating their leadership confidence.

In this event, Confident Communicator, you learn how communication is a confidence blocker or a builder. It can knock you down or knock you up a notch within your organization or with your clients, depending how you use all your senses to get what you want through sales, negotiations, or a business presentation. Effective leaders are typically effective communicators, but effective communicators are not necessarily effective leaders. Only by having the right balance will a leader become effective. Your consistent confidence will send a consistent communication of your leadership style.

John C. Maxwell, the great leadership guru and consultant, celebrated the tenth anniversary edition of his *New York Times* bestselling book, *The 21 Irrefutable Laws of Leadership.* In his second law, the "law of influence," he states, "The true measure of leadership is influence—nothing more, nothing less." This is a fact that cannot be disputed! Without confidence in your ability to influence others, nothing can be done. By taking a customer-centric approach, encircled with core leadership attributes as the influencers, you can build on each strategic need of your business. To be able to influence, you must be able to effectively communicate internally and externally.

Portraying Confidence

There is nothing more important than the ability to express confidence through your communication.

Portraying confidence is having consistency in your confidence and knowing the following:

✓ Your actions are your messaging.

✓ Your communications represent your intent.

✓ Your body language helps tell the story.

✓ Your words, in print or in dialogue, communicate who you are and where you stand on a given issue.

✓ Your silence can tell it all.

Ram Charan, a well-known expert on business strategy and the author of *Leadership in the Era of Economic Uncertainty*, lists six essential leadership traits that are needed when businesses are facing hard times:

1. Honesty and credibility

2. The ability to inspire

3. Real-time connection with reality

4. Realism tempered with optimism

5. Managing with intensity

6. Boldness in building for the future

All six are interdependent and require the proper balanced attention and focus. These traits need to be effectively executed via formal meetings or one-on-one sessions. To execute these strategies of leadership, especially during those intense sessions, the leader must possess a strong level of confidence.

Can you imagine a leader of your organization coming to you or your team to talk about the difficult times the company is having and how it may impact you? If the leader is not talking honestly or is not credible, it shows through his or her low level of confidence. If the leader cannot confidently inspire the organization to stay with the team and work through a crisis, it will be difficult to retain the organization. The leaders' connection with reality is important, and they must be able to effectively convey their messaging by balancing their communication with optimistic realism. Managing with intensity and having audacious discussions on fearlessly building for the future requires leaders to communicate effectively and with self-confidence.

The three levels of confidence are self-confidence, overconfidence, and low confidence. As you read the descriptions below, think through your own leadership style and when or how you exhibit your level of confidence. Think through your feedback from your trusted advisers or 360 assessments and what you have learned. Think about the leaders, managers, and supervisors you have worked with, and create a quick mental checklist of who the key words remind you of. Think about why some leaders are overconfident while others are very self-confident or exhibit low confidence. Think through the drivers of each, and add your own if needed.

SELF-CONFIDENCE	OVERCONFIDENCE	LOW CONFIDENCE
Certainty	Arrogant	Confused
Courage	Egotistic	Dismayed
Determination	Pushy	Nervous
Trustful	Distrustful	Distrustful
Influential	Overly positive	Doubtful
Tenacity	Conceited	Suspicious
Reliable	Brash	Pessimistic

Resilient	Brazen	Boring
Reassuring	Cocky	Uncertain
Poise	Pretentious	Hesitant
Stable	Unflappable	Doubting
Influential	Influential	Weak
Leadership	Careless	Low self-esteem
_____	_____	_____
_____	_____	_____

ASK: What level of confidence do you exhibit? Is it consistent? If not, what are the gaps that need to be balanced? What or how do you improve?

These levels of confidence and the descriptors are labels put on us by the "messaging" we send. The messaging comprises the events of our actions and our communications to others. Confident communication is to become balanced in how you view yourself versus how others view you. You want to communicate your confidence level effectively so that the receiver understands the same message of confidence.

Your messaging of confidence should be received and mirrored as a measure of your confidence. The balancing of your confidence level must mirror how you want the receiver to understand your actions. This is what I call balanced messaging, and it is demonstrated in the figure below.

Balanced Messaging

Your messaging of confidence
should be received and mirrored
as a measure of your confidence

There is an old saying that "you are what you say, and what you say, you portray." If your confidence level is not being communicated with the intent you mean, you are off balance. If your actions are not in line with what you say, you portray the wrong balanced confidence.

I knew a general manager who consistently demonstrated an unbalanced confidence level. His name was Ronald, and he worked for a large, international Fortune 500 organization. He was a leader in the making and soon to be named vice president of his company's global services division. He was ambitious, pushed the envelope with his superiors to get things done, and was viewed as a risk-taking leader. He had the right executive presence, was a great presenter of data, and communicated up the chain well but suffered when it came to communicating to his staff and his first-line teams. He was good, but he exhibited his insecurities by keeping a tight-knit group of followers by his side. These followers were not trusted advisers of the business but trusted advisers for his ego. He had all the signs of overconfidence. His peers viewed him as cocky, arrogant, and distrustful. However, he viewed himself as portraying an aura of knowledge. He was great in spinning the politics of corporate life, but he was also known for being manipulative in his actions.

Ronald wore his mood on his shoulders, good or bad, and was overconfident one day and displayed low-confidence the next. When he did not get his way, his confidence level failed him.

Ronald needed consistency, but his overconfidence made him rely on his political power base to keep him going and progressing up the ranks. In the end, he came to realize that his imbalanced confidence had to be controlled in order for him to continue to succeed. Balanced confidence must be consistent!

It took an event for Ronald to recognize that his over-the-top arrogance had to stop if he wanted the vice president's role. The event was on a personal level and was strong enough for him to step back and become more humble. All who knew him recognized how the event changed him. Still, it was not until he removed himself from his so-called trusted advisers and began trusting the feedback of his peers and senior leadership team that he recognized his full potential.

I need to make a point about a lower level of confidence that I call "blind confidence." At times, this is also called "stupid confidence," which is smart people doing or making stupid remarks that affect who they are as a leader. Don't get caught up in your own view of your confidence level or the confidence levels of others. Blind confidence can attack at all three levels. Blind confidence is a combination of all three taken to the extreme, leading to over-the-top measures and decisions based only on your trust or loyalty to the leaders you follow. Ronald exhibited certain levels of blind confidence, but he was consistently overconfident and independently influential with senior executives. However, he surrounded himself with a staff of leaders who exhibited blind confidence by thinking that they would always be protected by their loyalty to him.

Blind confidence typically happens to individual contributors and managers who blindly believe in their overconfident leader. If you made that mental list, you may have thought of times when leaders, or even you, let blind confidence overwhelm a sense of direction. Blind confidence is when you feel you can do no wrong, when you are caught misreading someone's character, or when you judge people wrongly because you feel it is politically right to do so. Blind confidence or stupid confidence can exist in many leaders, and it can be eliminated only when they consistently ask for trustworthy feedback.

The Confident Communicator

As previously stated, "Your messaging of confidence should be received and mirrored as your message of confidence." The key is to position your messaging so that it is effective, meaning that your messaging is in your communication abilities. To exhibit a balanced confidence level, you must have the ability to inspire and influence, which means that you need to be able to effectively communicate. We are going to dig in and demonstrate how to effectively communicate to an audience.

Here are some facts on communication based on a study conducted at the University of Pennsylvania ("Kinesics and Communications," Ray Birdwhistell):

- Seven percent of what we communicate is the result of the words that we say or the content of our communication.

- Thirty-eight percent of our communication to others is a result of our verbal behavior, which includes tone of voice, timbre, tempo, and volume.

- Fifty-five percent of our communication is a result of our nonverbal communication, body posture, skin color, and movement. (Birdwhistell, 1985)

The match between nonverbal and verbal communication indicates the level of congruency. If effective communication is the exhibition of confidence, it is not just what you say but how you say it! Let's build confidence by focusing on the 93 percent, and the 7 percent will follow.

ASK: How does your communication skill hold up? How effective of a communicator do you think you are? What does your feedback tell you? Do you already know the areas of communication that you need to improve?

As a paid public speaker, I recognize the value of using both verbal and nonverbal cues to effectively communicate. I conduct workshops and seminars that teach people how to communicate and present ideas in a professional demeanor. When working with small groups, the focus is more on what is *not* said than on what is said. I am also an active member of my local Toastmasters International club, where I mentor professionals in the art of public speaking.

Toastmasters International club draws in professionals because they received feedback from their employers that they should develop their communication skills to better their careers and advance within the company. As an executive coach and trainer of coaches, I spend a lot of time working with clients on leadership traits that need to be developed through effective communication. I also work with people who are trying to remove their fear of public speaking. This fear is a weakness that exhibits low confidence. It does not surprise me that the fear of public speaking, to many, ranks second to the fear of death.

Before I present a detailed guide on how to develop effective and confident communications, I want to clarify three points.

1. "Communication is power!" As Anthony Robbins states in his famous book *Unlimited Power*, "Those who have mastered its effective use can change their own experience of the world and the world's experience of them."

   a. I believe in Robbins's assessment that we produce two forms of communication. First, we conduct internal communications: those things we picture, say, and feel within ourselves. Second, we experience external communications: words, tonalities, facial expressions, body postures, and physical actions that communicate with the world.

   b. Knowing this helps you recognize how important communication is—not just for organization leaders but for anyone trying to exhibit confidence and influence, inspire, or persuade others to follow.

   c. You are always communicating, and they (the listeners) are always communicating with you!

2. Conquer your fear of public speaking.

   a. If you have this fear, you know that your fear is real. You created it at some time in your life and may believe that it cannot be removed. As long as you believe this, you will always have this fear!

b. Understand that you created the fear, and only you can remove it. As long as you believe that you can remove it, you will overcome it!

c. When you speak to an audience, understand that it is not about you. It is about the audience. It takes practice and time to remove this fear, but it can be controlled if you want to control it. Believe that you can!

3. Learning how to effectively present and speak in public will lift your career!

a. If this is what you believe, then it may well happen, although there are never any guarantees.

b. There are plenty of brilliant historical leaders and leaders within organizations who are labeled poor speakers, just as there are plenty of great speakers who are poor leaders. My example, Ronald, was a dominant, influential speaker but not a consistent leader.

c. Learning how to effectively present and speak in public will lift your confidence and leave an impression of confidence with the audience. Becoming an effective speaker opens doors for many, but after that, other traits must be applied.

With the proper consistent training, I firmly believe that public speaking fears can be removed, and everyone can train to develop the craft of public speaking. Some speakers, as with leaders, are born, and some need to be trained. It may take an event for you to recognize that you have the ability and the belief that will drive your will.

To further clarify these points, I use an example of the work I did with a client named Angie. Angie had panic attacks each time she had to deliver a business presentation to her superiors. A well-educated MBA graduate from a prestigious university, she communicated openly and easily one on one, but when it came to standing up in front of an audience, she was nauseated and unable to speak. For years she relied on one of her colleagues to step in for her, but that came to a halt. She knew that she needed to step up, because while she could potentially hide from presenting internally within the company, she had to do formal customer presentations, and she was not ready. She prepared herself over and over to conduct a presentation for a small group of potential clients, and right before the event, she canceled. Embarrassed by an event that almost cost her her job, she decided to seek help.

We created five areas to help develop her public speaking ability, and I added five more. (I continue to use these ten as the foundation for my workshops and speaking seminars.) Angie is now comfortable with speaking to small or large audiences. She has what we all typically have—a sense of nervousness before each speaking event—but she easily recovers as she communicates her message with utmost confidence.

Confident Communicator Guide

Communication is power, so let's begin!

1. **Serve the audience.** It is not about you; it is about the audience that wants to learn about the information you are sharing. As a speaker, it is all about providing the listeners with the right information and material they seek. You have a responsibility to share it and to share it with confidence. When you deliver the information correctly, the audience is obligated to receive the information and understand it. You are the messenger, and you

are there to serve the audience with information. You serve the audience no differently from how actors on stage are there to perform for their audience or how a comedian with his or her list of jokes or funny stories is there for one purpose—to make other people laugh—not for himself. The expressions and how the comedian says the punch lines make or break the jokes. It is the same when you serve your audience: you provide them with the information they need to learn. Serve them well with passion, emotion, humor, seriousness, and confidence. You have been in the audience and know what you would like to hear or feel from a speaker. Step into the shoes of an audience member, and deliver your material the way you would want to receive it. Serve the audience members by talking to them. Make it personal even when sharing data or metrics; bring them into the conversation by hitting on points of interest and facts.

Angie was great in creating her presentation slides because she knew her information. She was the subject matter expert, but when she created slides, she did not create them with the audience in mind. She did not envision herself standing in front of her peers or customers and delivering the information; she just laid out the facts. Once she built her confidence, she created slides with the audience in mind. The slides went from great to brilliant. She kept the audience in mind and delivered.

2. **The use of role modeling.** As described in event two, using role modeling to develop your skills as a leader or speaker is one of the best ways to perfect your abilities. Effective leaders have used this method for years because it works. If you have attended a meeting, a workshop, or a banquet that had a keynote speaker that you were impressed by, you have an opportunity to emulate

what that speaker did to capture your attention. It works in the opposite way as well. If the speaker turned you off and did not capture you or most of the audience, recognize what he or she did wrong, and make sure that you do not make the same mistakes. Capture the lessons of the speaker and note, or even memorize, what the speaker did to successfully gain your attention.

The primary role model that we used to help Angie develop her speaking abilities was Lisa Nichols, a famous public speaker, motivator, and the author of *Chicken Soup for the African American Woman's Soul*. When Angie told me that Nichols was who she aspired to become, I was impressed by the bar she set for herself because Nichols is an extremely polished speaker, but I knew her story. She had to train and develop her motivational speaking voice. I asked Angie to write down the top five things she enjoyed about Nichols's method of speaking. I wanted to know what impressed or captured Angie most when she heard Nichols speak. When she sent me her list, I mapped some of the core senses that Nichols was appealing to:

1. Inspirational   (Appealing to feelings)

2. Storytelling   (Appealing to hearing)

3. Speaks with passion   (Appealing to feelings)

4. Connects with the audience (Appealing to sight)

5. Direct eye contact to each (Appealing to sight)

As I worked with Angie, we looked at YouTube videos of Nichols conducting presentations, and Angie realized how Nichols appealed to the five senses. Specifically, they captured emotions. This is the perfect way to reach out to an audience, and it is part of the art of mirroring.

Using the senses to capture the audience through their senses makes the appropriate connection.

The traits that Angie found in Nichols can be found in any role model that you choose. You want to speak and have command of the audience as exhibited by the person you choose. Pick out the person's traits, practice them, use your senses to appeal to the audience's senses, and get feedback on your progress. Mirror the tone and use of expressions. What works for the person may work for you. Customize what you feel fits your personality. Observe the body language and eye contact that draws the audience in, and take note of how the person speaks.

Refer to event one and use the five-step Mirror Map when seeking a role model to develop your public speaking skills. When you start modeling a leader's speaking ability, you may also find that you are modeling the person's leadership abilities.

3. **Use sensory channels.** Recognize that any event in our daily lives is processed through one or all of our sensory channels: sight (visual), hearing (auditory), touch (kinesthetic), smell (olfactory), and taste (gustatory). Using your sensory channels is critical because 55 percent of communication has been proven to come from nonverbal messaging. Using your senses as a communication vehicle applies, and using all or most of your five senses to appeal to your audience will take practice.

If you use emotion when you speak, it affects feelings. The audience empathizes with the speaker. You may have seen a speaker who walks into the room and puts a hand on an audience member's shoulders for the "touch" effect. Experienced leaders and salespeople know that touching the person they address by shaking hands or placing their hand on a shoulder demonstrates a feeling of trust. As the receiver of this touch, you gain a connection. Many professionals use a handshake, but instead of using one hand, they extend the other to hold the person's forearm, therefore affirming the connection between them.

Direct eye contact draws the audience in (sight). While you may not be able to have eye-to-eye contact with everyone in the room, looking to a specific section in the room or auditorium can broaden the eye connection. In a smaller setting, when stressing a point, making direct eye contact with as many people as you can makes a difference in their attention span. This also applies to what you wear when giving a speech. Don't wear anything that distracts the audience from your message. They are using their sense of sight, so how you move and use body language, as well as what you wear, are significant in how your audience will pay attention. At the same time, learn to watch the audience's body language, and watch how they react to what you are saying.

In the auditory (hearing) realm, a core element for successful speaking is your vocal tone. I have been in the room when high-ranking, respected leaders sounded like they were mumbling, leading me to believe that they couldn't hear themselves or that they had low confidence. Many leaders use little vocal emotion. For some leaders, this may not matter, because they are already effective influencers, but for most, "vocal variety" is a must. Think about when you listen to a speaker: which is more effective: a monotone speaker, or the speaker who uses vocal tone to stress the points? By far it is the one who has a command of vocal tone and expressions. Before presenting or speaking, test the venue to see how your voice projects across the room. Make sure that you are heard, and use vocal range to capture the attention of your audience. An effective speaker will listen to the audience members, hear what they are saying, and notice what they are not saying.

Using your senses of smell and taste is rare during business presentations, but when the presentation calls for them, use them to your full advantage. There are occasions when we use all five senses to capture an audience. One example is when you make a toast with a glass of wine. All are asked to raise their glasses and listen to the toastmaster give the toast. You smell the wine, your glasses touch and clink, and you all taste the wine in unison.

Using your sensory channels and connecting with the audience's sensory channels are highly beneficial for a speaker. The connection brings the right level of confidence and keeps the attention of the audience. This takes a lot of practice, so be patient when trying to use your senses to communicate, and continue to use role models as examples.

4. **Process and filtering.** Recognizing how you and your audience receive the information you are giving, and how they filter it, is a complete science that is worth mentioning. Like role modeling and using sensory channels to communicate, the art of processing and filtering of information was mastered by the originators of Neurolinguistic Programming (NLP), Richard Bandler and John Grinder, who developed it at the University of California at Santa Cruz in the mid-1970s. NLP at its core is about modeling human excellence, and it can help you produce a desired change or outcome in yourself. It is also the foundation of many of the practices and beliefs of Anthony Robbins. Although I am not a practitioner of NLP, I understand and use many of its concepts,

specifically in understanding how we process and filter everyday communication. I also use it for my awareness in public speaking.

Three distinct filters occur as we process the information we receive. I point these out because you can lose your audience every eight seconds. I want you to understand what is going on in the minds of the listeners. The filters we all experience are deletion, distortion, and generalization.

Deletion. The mind can process billions of bits of information, but we are unable to retain all that we consume on a daily basis. Just like your computer's hard drive, the mind needs to delete some information so that it can consume more. When you attend an event and want to focus on the speaker, you condition yourself to focus and delete any distractions that may occur. When reading a book, you may skim over (or delete) some of the words or letters. When you listen to information, you may delete some of what was said and focus on what you consider the important parts to retain. As a speaker or a person communicating information, recognize that your audience can consume only parts of your information, so moderate what you are sharing. An example would be to slow down or repeat the point you are making to allow the listeners to decide what to delete in order to make room for new data. Good communicators know that the deletion filter is core to us, as listeners, so that we can process the new information provided.

Distortion. As a speaker, ensure that you speak in specifics so there is limited room for the listener to distort the information. Distorting information is common. We visualize a comment the speaker has said, map it to our own experience, and wander off to our personal beliefs rather than the belief of the speaker.

Listeners create their own meaning of what they hear. This also occurs when trying to read the body language of others. You may observe a person twitching or slouching as you speak and interpret this to mean that the person is disengaged. This is your own interpretation, and it may be distorted. The person may have been trying to scratch an itch or was bothered by a bad back. The distortion filter can work for you or against you as it puts your imagination to work. As a speaker, recognize that your audience members may be using this filter to gather the information that applies to them and distorting the rest.

Generalization. This filter, much like deletion and distortion, can work for you or against you. Generalization is the basis of assumptions you can make when a speaker or presenter is not specific. When you are not specific, there is plenty of room for the listener to try to "read into" what you are saying. As an example, a comment such as "It is always hot in Texas, so be sure to dress appropriately" is based only on your experience. Listeners will create their own images in their minds. Perhaps when they visited Texas it was during an ice storm, causing their flight to be delayed. This filter can be dangerous especially when giving solutions or remedies to problems. To avoid generalization, it would be best to say, "It is always hot in Texas in July and August, so be sure to dress appropriately."

As with deletions and distortions, if you are not specific, listeners will wander off into their own beliefs or experiences. As a speaker, stay specific and give examples to limit the listeners' own beliefs.

Processing and filtering can be illustrated by the childhood game some of you may recall as "Telephone." Everyone sits in circles of five or more. The game begins with one person whispering a short story to the person beside him. That person then repeats it to the next person, and so on. As the story makes its way around the circle, it becomes distorted; some information is deleted, and some is generalized with others' experiences or understanding of the story. These are the internal filters that exist as we take in information. As a speaker, the more you know how your information is being filtered and processed, the better you will be as a speaker.

In NLP, there are several more filters that determine what we delete, distort, and generalize. These are in-depth understandings based on your values, beliefs, memories, decisions, and what NLP coaches call "meta programs" or filters that determine how you perceive the world around you.

For more information on NLP, there are hundreds of books to refer to, but for building your communication competence, knowing these three filters should assist in creating effective messaging.

5. **The "Tells" and the "Threes."** These are simple process rules of understanding the flow of communication and the importance of being succinct. The rule of the "tells" is as follows: Tell the audience what you are going to tell them. Tell them, and then tell them what you told them. This is the beginning, the middle, and the recap at the end.

The Tells

a. Tell them what you are going to tell them. When beginning your presentation or speech, first inform the audience of the information you are going to share. It is a preview or snapshot of the content. Using this as an introduction or hook to bring the audience in by letting them know what you are going to talk about keeps their attention with you. Be careful not to give too much detail or facts or allow your presentation to bleed over to part (b) of your presentation. Say what you are going to tell them with some information on why you are going to share the information with them.

Example: *Today I am going to share with you three primary needs of our business strategy that are critical to our business growth. They are, one, focus on product and profitability, two, grow market share through new innovation, and three, develop our people through new training and development programs. These strategy points are crucial to our success.*

b. Tell them. Upon completing part a, you begin to tell them. This part contains the facts, the details, and the meat of your presentation or speech. (When we get to step 6 of this section, you will learn how to be precise in giving information in a clearly processed format.) In this area, this is your story! In part (a), you have primed the storyline, but now is the time to give the specifics. This is what your audience came to hear, so be detailed, and provide the facts, data, and all the relevant information of your storyline or presentation.

Example: *Let me begin with the first point: focus on product and profitability.*

c. Tell them what you told them. This is the recap and ending part of the process. Like any recap, it is an opportunity to reinforce the information you shared. You can stress the key points you mentioned during your introduction, reminding the audience of the information you shared. This can also be used to emphasize the benefits of the information or the key points of the content.

Example: *In conclusion, these three focal points for our business strategy are critical to our business growth for the reasons I described, but most importantly, they fill the need for our organization to continue to grow. Focusing on our product and profitability, growing market share through innovation, and developing our people through new training and development programs will ensure that we maintain a competitive edge.*

This rule is used in most literature, speeches, and presentations, and as in each step of this book, practice is required to build your comfort level. When preparing a speech or presentation, review the process: "Tell them what you are going to tell them, tell them, and then tell them what you told them!"

The Threes

To help you work with how people filter and process information, I recommend using the "politician's rule" of simplifying presentations or speeches to three or four points that you want the audience to remember. I call it the politician's rule because most politicians sum up their answers to questions in three or four key points. (In most cases, when they respond, they are not even sure what the three or four points are, but as they process their information, the second or third points follow.)

The process of The Threes helps when you repeat or stress three points of a statement. Using three points brings attention to your message. Read how these famous statements catch our attention:

- "I came, I saw, I conquered."

- "Friends, Romans, countrymen."

- "The good, the bad, the ugly."

- "He was tall, dark, and handsome."

- "Government of the people, by the people, for the people."

- "Our mission is at once the oldest and the most basic of this country: to right wrong, to do justice, to serve man!"

Each statement uses three key or repetitive words to bring a strong impact to the message.

6. **STARR and the Six-Step Process.** To further form your speech or presentation in a succinct manner, here are two important processes to follow. Depending on the information you present, you will know which approach to use. Both communication tools are used in a variety of businesses, but they seem to get lost in today's fast-paced communication processes.

STARR

STARR stands for Situation, Task, Accomplishments, Results, and Recommendations. This verbal or written form of communication is used when you need to get right to the point of an issue. Many leaders use this type of communication to inform clients of the status of the business or an issue they are addressing.

- Situation. Describe the current situation you, your team, or your company is working on. This is a status update of where you are with an issue, problem, or opportunity.

- Task. Describe what you, your team, or your company has been doing to address the situation or problem. Be specific on the exact tasks or process going on behind the scenes. This is an opportunity to be informative.

- Accomplishments. You have described the task that you, your team, or company has been doing, so now describe what was accomplished. This is usually in a bullet format and is an opportunity to praise or recognize the work that was done.

- Results. Describe the outcome of your task and accomplishments. Report the final results or status of the work you, your team, or your organization completed. Be specific, and be sure to provide a graphic showing a direct correlation between the situation (problem), task completed and its outcome.

- Recommendation. Give your overall recommendations based on the accomplishments and results or findings. This may be a task for the audience or a to-do list, and it can be used as an as-needed step.

The Six-Step Process

This is an in-depth communication vehicle that I often use for written or verbal proposals. It is good to use for PowerPoint presentations. While similar to STARR, the Six-Step Process offers details on how to solve an issue or address a problem. This is a good way to sell a program or a product, and it has been referred to as the "Six-Step Selling Process" due to the persuasive tone it can have. It is a positive approach to share your thinking process with the audience.

1. Current situation. Like STARR, begin by describing the current status of the issue, problem, or opportunity. This sets the foundation of the state of the business or issue you are going to address.

2. Key issues. These issues should be listed as questions related to the situation and broken out as questions (How can we…? How will we…? What needs to be done…? Can we…?).

3. Solution or recommendation. Respond to the key issues on how you will resolve the issues. This is the solution or recommendation that you are suggesting.

4. How it works. Describe how your solution or recommendation will work. This could be a process change and/or a call to action.

5. Benefits. Talk about he key benefit to your solution and how it works. Identifying the benefit may repeat some of the solutions, but be sure to identify the benefits for the key stakeholders involved.

6. Next steps. Describe specifically the call to action. What are the specific next steps that need to be taken?

The Six-Step Process allows you to put in as much detail as needed, and it typically addresses the right level of information. Using the Six-Step Process for the first time may be cumbersome, but it brings the right level of confidence when presented with confidence.

7. **Affirmation.** Effective speakers keep their audience drawn in by including them in the conversation and asking for confirmation of

what they have been told. Affirmation is formed as a question that does not necessarily need to be answered. As the speaker, you are looking for the validity of your statement. Affirmation asserts that something exists or is true, and when you are speaking on a topic, use affirmation to gain approval and maintain the attention of the audience.

Here are a few examples of affirmations. These types of statements are best used once you have detailed the material you are presenting:

- Do you agree?

  o "Do you agree that our three-point strategy will bring the right level of confidence to most of our stakeholders?"

- Do you follow?

  o "If we want to win this sales opportunity, we need to create a presentation that is both impactful and informative. Do you follow?"

- Are you with me?

  o "Gaining the board's approval to create a move-forward strategy in each of the areas outlined will put us on target for our December 30 deadline. Are you with me?"

- Do you feel?

  o "Do you feel the same way I do? Do you feel that our next quarter sales initiatives will have a higher impact?"

All four examples demonstrate how the audience is drawn in and affirms your statement or question. You have given the facts, and now you are confirming their buy-in through their affirmation of what you are saying. This technique will take practice, but depending on what you are presenting, it is a great tool to use to further the acceptance of your material.

8. **Use the heart.** You have heard the phrases "Let's have a heart-to-heart conversation" or "I am going to speak from the heart" or "We had a heartfelt discussion." You have probably used these statements yourself or have been involved in these types of conversations. When you say that you are going to speak from the heart, it implies that you are going to have a serious and truthful conversation. The listeners ready themselves to be engaged with what you have to say. In some cases, you are telling them to ready their own hearts, because what you are going to share with them is important, direct, and perhaps personal. As the speaker, you will be open to let out what you want to say, and as the listener, you will be open to what you are about to hear.

In my example of Angie's admiration for how Lisa Nichols spoke to her audience, each of the five areas that stood out reached Angie's sensory channels. The most important sensory channel a speaker can reach is feelings. This is what elegant speakers such as Nichols have mastered; they can speak to the heart, from theirs to yours! The key takeaway Angie had about Lisa's speaking ability was that it was inspirational, told a story, spoke with passion, connected with the audience, and gave direct eye contact. Think about a time when you had a heart-to-heart conversation with someone. These five areas were probably used in that heartfelt conversation, and it is the same when speaking to a group.

When stressing a point to your audience or when you want to speak with passion and exhibit trust and confidence, speak from the heart. Tell the audience beforehand, if you like, that you are going to make a statement from the heart so that the audience prepares to listen. Speaking from the heart allows the audience to resonate with what you are saying and creates the high level of connection.

9. **Know the room.** One of the major issues leaders have is that they don't take the time to know the room before they speak. They don't know who their audience is or why the audience is there. To connect, command the room, and build true rapport with the audience, a good speaker must always know some of the background and needs of the audience. It allows you to adapt your communication style to one that encourages audience participation. Knowing the room and building rapport with an audience builds trust and confidence and creates the relationship you need to keep the audience in tune.

When I began my career with Microsoft, I was in charge of developing a partner program for the services organization for the Latin America region. At the time, Microsoft had offices in Mexico, Panama, Costa Rica, Puerto Rico, Venezuela, Peru, Colombia, Chile, Brazil, and Argentina. I brought all of the services leads from these offices to Dallas for our first strategy meeting. I also brought in senior leaders from our corporate offices in Redmond to present the overall global strategy. All together, we had eighteen executives in the room from the US and Latin America. This was the first time our Latin American and corporate delegates had met and the first time I recognized that we had some opportunities to work on diversity. Primarily, though, we had communication issues.

The corporate leads came well prepared and excited to meet and work with their Latin American counterparts, but their presentations and dialogue were designed for a US audience. While most Microsoft employees are required to speak English, the first language of these people was Spanish or Portuguese. During our introductions, the Americans had difficulty pronouncing many of the Spanish and Portuguese names and asked to use a shorter name or even a nickname. This was embarrassing, because the Latin American team did not ask the US teams to use shorter names. Our first US presenter started with PowerPoint slides and gave analogies using famous US sports athletes, specifically US football players, not realizing that American football exists only in the US. He used US-centric colloquialisms, which was all jargon to our Latin American guests. He talked about how our strategy had to be like a "quarterback sneak" (meaning to surprise an opponent in football when the quarterback runs the ball), and he asked the team to "sit tight" as he readjusted his slide presentation. After that comment, our Latin American friends did not know which way to sit. It went on like this until our break. I asked the US team members to become more cognizant of their choice of words, but even then, they could not break their habits. As they gave their presentation, they continued to use colloquialisms, and if they caught themselves, they got derailed by explaining what the slang or colloquialism meant.

Knowing your audience from a diversity perspective includes language and geographic differences. Some presenters may talk humorously about a bad experience in a city or country, not knowing that 50 percent of the audience is from that location, which can create a disconnection between them and the audience. It is critical for presenters to know the diversity of technical competency, topic knowledge, and the information needs of the audience before they begin. Knowing some of the background of the audience helps you to involve them, allows you to bring value, and creates the needed rapport and connection.

Our US presenters could have built rapport with their Latin American colleagues by first conducting informal or formal conversations with the audience, finding out more about the countries they represented, and the challenges they were having in partner and strategy development. By having these conversations, they would have discovered the strength of their colleagues' command of the English language rather than assuming everyone was proficient in English. They might have discovered connections about the cities the audience members lived in or made connections regarding family, children, and ancestors. Knowing this information, the presenters could have tied these discoveries into their communications and created a personal touch, therefore keeping the audience engaged. Knowing the room, understanding the audience, and building connections, trust, and confidence will build the rapport to keep them engaged.

10. **Power listening.** Have you ever been in a meeting or a presentation, asked the speaker a question regarding the material, and heard an answer that was not relevant to your question? If you have, it means that the speaker is not listening, is thinking more of his or her presentation, or is distracted by other activity in the room. Have you ever sat in the audience bored to death by what the speaker was saying and began fidgeting about in your seat? The speaker, again, was not listening to your body language but was busy listening to himself or herself.

Power listening is about developing listening capabilities for verbal and nonverbal cues that come from the person you're speaking to. If you drift off and do not answer questions directly, you are sure to lose the confidence of the listener. If you are not able to read the audience members by their communication gestures, you can be labeled as an incompetent communicator.

Here are three points to help you become an effective power listener:

1. Pay attention. This seems simple enough, but our minds are fast-working machines, and our attention spans are limited. Condition yourself to stay focused on how the listener is communicating to you. It is important to note that you are always communicating, and the listeners are always communicating with you, so pay attention!

There are two levels of attention, focused and sustained, which typically work consecutively.

- *Focused attention* is a short-term response to a stimulus that attracts attention. The attention span for this is perhaps as short as eight seconds. An example is hearing a door close or a cellular phone ring. After it captures your attention, you go back to whatever task you were doing.

- *Sustained attention* is the level of attention that produces consistent results on a task over time. If your task is to put something (such as a jigsaw puzzle) together over a ten- to fifteen-minute period, you need to demonstrate sustained attention to stay on task. If you lose focus, you may mismatch pieces of the puzzle or lose track of the time needed to complete the task. Most healthy teenagers and adults are unable to sustain attention on one thing for more than forty minutes at a time, although they can choose to repeatedly refocus on the same thing. This ability to renew attention permits people to pay attention to things that last more than a few minutes such as a long movie or reading a book. Attention span, as measured by sustained attention or the time spent continuously on a task, varies with age.

Balancing your sustained and focused attention allows you to listen to verbal and nonverbal messaging. At Microsoft, a commonly used practice was: precise questions should lead to precise answers. If asked a question, focus on what the person is saying, repeat the question in your mind, or ask that the question be repeated. Be precise in your answer, and by building a sustained focus with your audience, you strengthen your attention to the details and build your power listening abilities.

2. Listen to the eyes. Yes, it is true! Even without saying one word, your eyes tell it all! Many of you have experienced that feeling of reading someone by the way the eyes move away from you, up or down, or the proverbial rolling of the eyes that demonstrates frustration or lack of interest. Your eye movement is a "tell," as many poker enthusiasts say. Poker players look for that twitch or shift in their opponents' eyes that expose whether they have a good or bad hand of cards. Some people exaggerate the truth by saying, "I can tell by your eyes that you're lying." Many NLP practitioners use eye movement patterns as indicators of what their clients may be thinking, and some have done extensive studies on what eye movements represent during communication. For the most part, we use our experience and instincts to help us determine this; reading other people's eye movements becomes second nature.

To enhance your power listening by listening to the eyes, pay attention to eye movements, and don't misread them. Recognize that listening is a two-way event, and use eye-to-eye contact when communicating.

Paying attention to eye movements can be developed over time and will create a full awareness of the messaging that may be occurring. If you are communicating with someone you know, you may already be able to read the response to what you said. During my extensive work with Angie, it was easy to notice when she disagreed with a comment. All those who knew her recognized that her eyes moved downward when she disapproved of a statement. If she was asked a question and her response was going to be negative, she subconsciously shifted her eyes downward before or while she responded.

When I brought this to her attention, it was clear that others knew her habit, but she did not. When we talked in further detail about reading eye movements, she felt that she was a master at reading people's eyes. I believed that she was a master. As I watched her working with others in her organization and during customer calls, she explained people's demeanor based solely on their eye movements. Typically, Angie was correct, but there was one instance before a sales call when she described one of her clients as "shifty eyed." In her interpretation, the client was not to be trusted. When I met the client, it was clear to me that he rapidly shifted his eyes back and forth, but my interpretation was that he did this when he seemed to be mentally gathering information. During my debriefing with Angie, we discussed this, and she claimed that she probably did misread his eye movements, as the client always exhibited a high level of trust. His shifting eyes communicated one thing to her and another to me. Misreading eye movement is common, and at times, you might get caught up in trying to be a mind reader based on what you interpret a person's eyes to be saying. If the eye pattern follows a behavioral pattern or reaction, your read may be correct, but if there is no historical pattern, you can rely on your instincts or wait for a pattern to develop.

3. Manage your information processing. As you begin power listening, you are taking in a lot of information. Your attention is focused on what the speaker is saying, so you have a lot to absorb. It is extremely easy to wander off into your own zone when the speaker hits a topic that resonates with you. When this happens, your mind connects with the event, and your memory goes off to a dream world, taking you to the place you experienced rather than listening to the experience of the speaker. In some cases, you may interrupt the speaker and begin telling him or her, your story or event. When this happens, you are not paying full attention to the speaker, and you are not managing or processing the information correctly. It is common to wander off into an historical event that was triggered by a comment, story, or word.

Josef, one of my colleagues at Microsoft, was a senior executive who had a deep technical and analytical mind. He was great with strategy and extremely good at presenting information to a small or large audience, but during one-on-one conversation, he could not manage his information processing. He constantly interrupted others when they spoke to the point that it was perceived as extremely rude. Because he was an executive, he did not receive the feedback he should have to help him stop this bad habit, but he was aware that the habit existed.

Observing Josef over the course of a week, I noticed that when the initiator of a conversation started to speak, typically to bring a concern or issue to him, Josef dominated the conversation and did not understand all the details of the information. As demonstrated by the graph below, which I reviewed with Josef, his interruptions were so common that he typically took over the conversation.

A speaker who began her conversation with Josef tried to move from point A to point B. (The speaker is represented by *S,* and Josef is represented by *J.*) When the speaker began, Josef got her derailed, off topic, or into an experience he had with the issue. When you get derailed it is also a form of story stealing. At point 3, both the speaker and Josef began a dialogue off topic that led to Josef derailing again (point 4) and ended with Josef dominating the conversation.

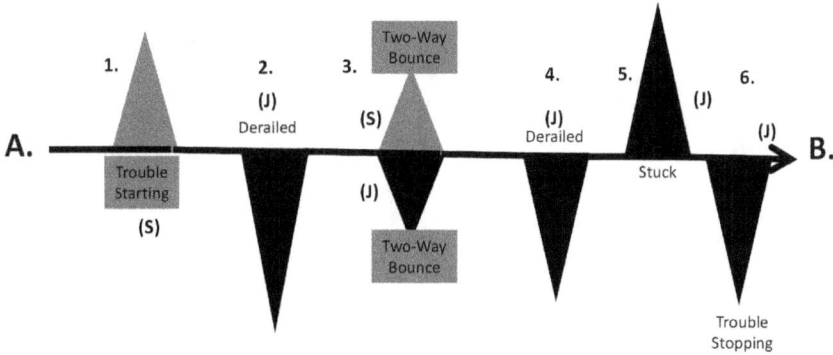

Josef did not have an attention deficit disorder, but he struggled with his process and filtering information as illustrated in step 6. When the three factors of filtering information—deletion, distortion, and generalization—are not balanced, it leads to these peaks and valleys of conversational derailment. As mentioned, you can lose your audience every eight seconds, and as the listener, you are the one who can get lost every eight seconds. Managing your information processing will help with your power listening.

To correct his processing of information, Josef began to take a notebook with him during one-on-one conversations, and rather than interrupt others, he wrote down his thoughts or questions. After the speaker completed the comment, Josef asked his questions or shared his findings. It led to balanced conversations, much to the credit of Josef, who wanted to balance his information processing.

When you hear a word, comment, or story that connects with you, process it, delete it, or mentally tuck it away to come back to after the speaker has finished. As a listener, you can distort and generalize the information you receive and focus on key points and issues. Listen with empathy, and take written and mental notes to come back to.

How to Lead It 2 Win It®

Event 4: Confident Communicator

Summary and Event Log

Examine your level of confidence, and understand how and when you need to increase or decrease it.

Get feedback from trusted advisers, and become more aware of how you display self-confidence.

Effective communication is the strongest asset a leader can bring to demonstrate, motivate, and inspire confidence.

What kind of communicator are you?

How do you listen?

What's your messaging?

Start developing your stakeholder awareness.

Build the confidence of your peer groups. Know that they are watching, and recognize the positive influence they bring.

EVENT 5
THE FIVE PRINCIPLES:
PRECISION, PLANNING, PRACTICE, PATIENCE, AND POSITIVITY

"All you need is the plan, the road map,
and the courage to press on to your destination."

EARL NIGHTINGALE

EVENT 5
THE FIVE PRINCIPLES:
PRECISION, PLANNING, PRACTICE, PATIENCE, AND POSITIVITY

Precision, planning, practice, patience, and positivity center on the ability to maneuver yourself to reach a specific desired state or goal. These principles can be applied when working on developing people, products, projects, or services. This subset of events follows a pattern that can keep you focused on what you have decided to do, how you are going to do it, and how repeating it will develop perfection, given the right time and attitude.

In a leadership role, it is critical to be as precise as possible when giving direction and setting goals or targets for yourself and others. You should have a clear plan on how to achieve these goals and practice enduring the level of patience needed for results to take effect. All five principles coincide, because each one carries the same significance, especially in maintaining a healthy, positive environment and approach.

As your self-development or leadership of people, projects, or services is in motion, the onus is on you to take full accountability and be consistent in achieving your goals for yourself, your community, or your professional organization. You own the responsibility to keep the business on a precise course. You own your business, department, district, or division. Whether you are an independent business owner or part of a large corporation, the accountability to make precise decisions and plans will fall on you. Having the right level of patience for results to take effect must be factored into your planning stage.

The event of these five principles resonated with me when I was introduced to how to develop strategic marketing and business plans for my sales organization. During the first part of the year, the company brought the entire sales organization together for a week that was dedicated to creating our business "game plans." We used the standard college lessons of inspecting external and internal aspects of the business.

The external factors of the business were the business environment, customer needs, and the competition. The four internal factors to examine were the organization needs, cross-functional needs, productivity, and finance/budgets. When working with organizations that were going through a change or merger/acquisition, I typically followed this format, examining each area to determine the right move-forward strategy. This gave us the precision and planning we needed.

The mantra our sales team had was "plan your work, and work your plan," and so we did with the commitment and persistence of every level of the organization. All understood the importance of working with a plan and recognized how to adapt the plan as needed. What the organization lacked was the ability to be patient as strategies unfolded.

As I developed proficiencies in creating business marketing plans, I got further involved with Project Management Institute, which zeros in on the disciplines of larger project planning. Using the same principles for personal development and business development, I set the goals and structured the processes to hit the target.

In the example of attributes and traits, I mentioned the courage seen in Linda, the district sales director from Northern California. While it took courage to fight for support, Linda was asking for the leadership's team to have patience in waiting for the market share results to come in. Her courage and request for patience paid off, and the lesson was that patience brought in the bonus payoff for the sales district.

Six months after Linda's display of courage, I joined her and a handful of other district managers to create our company's first leadership succession planning process. We agreed to create development plans for our managers to follow with their staff using the same concepts and disciplines we used in creating marketing and business plans. Linda was the first to ensure that we include key, measureable timelines for the personal development plans as well as a measurable range for key areas to be fully developed. Leadership competencies such as developing interpersonal awareness, impact and influence, organizational ability, and building confidence took time. As leaders, we had to create the road map with persistence and patience in mind. The leadership succession planning proved favorable, and the process we put in place remained for years thereafter.

This sales organization put in effort and time to create a business strategy and a people strategy. Like any noteworthy business, clear precision plans must be created to ensure success. It is the same with personal leadership development; it will mature with time and experience. Leadership is an ongoing practice, and by developing a chart showing personal or business strengths, weakness, opportunities, and threats, you target precise areas to build your skills or services.

The following section breaks down the five principles, which will help you with your road map. When you begin with precision, planning, practice, patience, and positivity in mind, you will end where you expect to be: right at the top of your game!

Coinciding Ps

Precision, planning, practice, patience, and positivity coincide because each one carries the same weight of importance. All five can occupy the same space, point in time, and/or relative position.

Precision

There is a clear distinction between accuracy and precision. People who were in the military or are familiar with playing darts or archery may know the difference between the two. In the example below, the marksmanship of an archer or bowman is developed by mastering the precision of clustering or grouping. Once this is done, the person focuses on developing skill at hitting the bull's eye of the target with accuracy. The arrows closest to the bull's eye are considered more accurate, while the arrows clustered together identify precision.

High **precision**,but low **accuracy**   High **accuracy**, but low **precision**

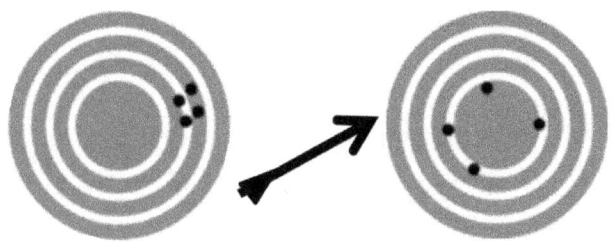

The target is an analogy for leadership, and knowing that the target and bull's eye is always moving, developing, growing, or changing, your objective is to develop your precision first. Accuracy may be temporarily low, but with practice and patience, both will come together.

As a leader, you must be precise in your communications, decisions, objectives, and direction. When measuring precision, scientists and technicians use the terms *repeatability* and *reproducibility*.

- Repeatability is the variation that occurs when repeated efforts are made by a single person or instrument. Like the clustering of the arrow, your leadership must have the repeatability to produce the same result. It takes constant, repeatable practice and diligence to create a leadership cluster.

- Reproducibility is the variation arising in the same measurement process but with different personnel or instruments and over longer periods of time. Reproducing the same results or quality of leadership in an organization despite the diversity of the leader requires skill and patience. To duplicate or reproduce, be precise in your training, communications, and direction of others.

You can use these analogies to build leadership repeatability and reproducibility to create precision for yourself and those you lead. You own the responsibility to navigate your career, the careers of others, and the business you are responsible for. Like the pilot of an airplane or the captain of a ship, a leader's precision in navigation is critical.

When developing or changing a behavior, be precise in the area that needs to develop or change. If you are developing your communication style, be detailed or precise on the specifics of what you want to improve, or you can become derailed and work on an area that is not as significant to your development. If you are building confidence levels, be precise on all that it entails such as your interpersonal skills, attire, and/or communications. Precision in your personal development is the foundation of what you need to change. Seek out your trusted advisers, coaches, or mentors, validate the important areas, and create your development plan.

Planning

The mantra of "plan your work, and work your plan" was introduced to me when I was running a sales organization, and I did not realize that it would be engrained in me forever. It has been the basis of how I engage in every facet of business I have been involved with. Project management principles or game plans draw out the strategic blueprint to build a product, process, technology, and service, and they are used effectively to create a people strategy. A leader cannot function without knowing or creating a planned road map. You are the person everyone turns to for direction. When you are asked by your superiors or team "What's the plan?" you had better have an answer. In my experience, it feels great when you have the answer and incredibly demoralizing when you don't.

In the 1990s when Bill Gates was still running Microsoft, he set a precedent on how to drill down into business planning metrics. David Thielen, who wrote *The 12 Simple Secrets of Microsoft Management*, described how Gates called his vice presidents on Saturday mornings and spent half an hour discussing the issues in their departments. Gates was known for drilling deep into every issue and metric, and he expected his vice presidents to have a plan behind their explanation. This precedent trickled down the chain of command from Gates to his vice presidents, general managers, directors, and so on. While I never presented my monthly planning updates to Gates, I presented to the Latin American vice president, who was just as masterful as Gates in getting to the crux of the matter.

During my first planning session at Microsoft, it was clear how unprepared I was regarding the details that the vice president requested. After an hour of grueling questioning, I left demoralized, beat up, feeling dizzy and sick, and thinking, *"What the heck just happened?"* I thought the questioning had derailed me from sharing the details of my plan, but the reality was that my plan was not strong enough to support the questioning. Little did I know that this was part of my initiation on how things worked at Microsoft! The next time I presented, I was more nervous, but the vice president and I were in sync with my planning and the way I presented the business. We were expected to know the metrics, the drivers behind each, and the plan to achieve expected goals. At every level, these sessions could be brutal if you did not know the details of your business or you could not articulate the details of your plans. This was also a clear demonstration of where precision and planning coincided. The Latin American vice president expected us all to have precise plans on how we were bringing value to the business, and so it went as we discussed our plans: expect precision questioning, and be prepared to provide precise answers.

Proper planning prevents poor performance. (There is typically another *P* included in this phrase, but you get the picture.) Planning is essential to anything you build, and without it your performance can suffer. Your product, services, and technology are all affected if proper planning and tracking are not in place. There are hundreds of websites to find templates on creating business, project, or game plans. Most major companies have their own format or will use PMI practices to create a go-forward strategy. If there is more complexity, high-cost association, and multiple stakeholder involvement such as working through a merger or acquisition, using a PMI practitioner is highly suggested.

Planning for your personal development requires the same thoughts, timelines, and key measurable areas as a plan you create for a business. In a business plan, you target areas to build your business. In a personal development plan, you target areas to build your personal brand. Precision will give you the areas to focus on and plan for milestones in the areas you want to develop. "Plan your work, and work your plan," and then seek feedback on your expected results. Proper planning will prevent low performance, so plan it out, seek it out, and work it out.

Practice

I cannot give a better example of practice than the findings in Malcolm Gladwell's book, *Outliers*. In chapter two, "The 10,000-Hour Rule," Gladwell outlines how persistence and practice create expertise, leading to perfection. He asks, "Is there such a thing as innate talent?" His findings indicate that there is but that the innately talented ones practice, practice, practice. Achievement, Gladwell writes, is talent plus preparation and practice. The ten thousand-hour rule is the time dedicated to practicing to become proficient in anything you do. *Outliers* gives examples of Bill Gates, who while at the University of Washington ran up 1,575 hours of computer time in seven months, which averaged eight hours a day, seven days a week. Through his research, Gladwell found that when Gates dropped out of Harvard after his sophomore year, he'd been programming practically nonstop for seven consecutive years. He was way past ten thousand hours.

Practice makes perfect? Not really, but good practice can make perfection. When you are trying to start, stop, or continue doing something, it will take repeatability and reproducibility, which means it takes a lot of practice to gain perfection. Habits are created because of repeatability and reproducibility, and the more you do, the more you get. As the saying goes, "If you always do what you've always done, you will always get what you've always got."

Every professional recognizes the advantages of practice. Sports professionals practice to master the game, the race, and the challenge. Spelling champions practice before they compete. Before a speech, politicians practice, trapeze artists practice the art of balance, and so on. When you are trying to master a change or develop a technique, it comes with the proper amount of dedicated practice. The more time you put into your practice, the more you build into the change you want to start, stop, or continue doing. Without practice, there will be no change to your personal development. Practice builds confidence, and good practice builds perfection. Practice the change, and the change will come.

Patience

I start with this quote taken from Leo Tolstoy, the famous Russian writer and poet: "The two most powerful warriors are patience and time." If you have been precise in thinking about your business goals or personal attributes, you are developing. If you have a well-thought-out plan with a specific and measurable timeline, the next thing to do is to factor in time and patience for change.

Having the right level of patience to demonstrate results has been proven beneficial in most facets of sports, personal training, and self-development. With time, repeatability, and reproducibility in practicing and measuring results, an athlete can demonstrate faster speeds when running a marathon or lifting heavier weights when strength training. The measurement of miles or weights over a six-week period should demonstrate positive progression. An athlete should not be expected to run a marathon or lift three times more weight after two or three weeks of training. If the athlete planned for nine weeks of training and was not derailed, he or she should be given the time to work the plan.

From a leadership perspective, you or your organization must be fully convinced that your repeatability and reproducibility will endure over time. As you work toward your goals, you may not see results in the first or second week. They may not measure up until the final weeks of a nine-week plan. Work the plan and be patient, and work the plan and be patient again. If the planning was precise, the results will be as expected. If adjustment is needed, adjust, measure, and be patient.

If patience is the companion of wisdom, leaders must be patient with their teams' results, and they need to convince others to become patient with their own. In the fast-paced, competitive business world, patience is the virtue that is the hardest to endure, especially if there are profits to be gained or lost. We all chase profit margins and market share, and we want results and want them now! Whether it's retail, services, or technology sales, there is a constant push to show what you have done lately.

The push today is to promote the multiplying and compounding effect through patient leadership. This creates a concentrated strength that can yield the desired results. Leaders should focus on proper planning, excellence in executing the plans, and effectively communicating the status of the plan. When the plans are right, the leaders should become the warriors to fight for enough time and have the patience for results to come in.

Leadership development requires you to be patient. Developing leadership qualities takes practice and time for competencies to mature. Don't expect change to happen during your first or second week of practicing a competency. Be patient with your diligence, and results will come.

ASK: When have you used precision planning to set business or personal goals? What is your level of patience about seeing expected results from yourself or others?

Positivity

Negative energy brings negative results, and positive energy brings positive results. As Henry Ford said, "If you believe you cannot, you will not." A leader can be the person in charge of others or of a business, but without a positive vision or positive environment, you or your organization will not prevail. What sports or executive coach motivates a team or an organization with negativity? There are some who use the method of "breaking the spirit" of people or a bad habit and building them up with a better behavior or habit. In the business world, there are some negative leaders who act positive only when their superiors are around.

The famous guru of positivity, Norman Vincent Peal, wrote *The Power of Positive Thinking.* Let me present some of his thought-provoking quotes:

"Believe in yourself! Have faith in your abilities! Without a humble but reasonable confidence in your own powers you cannot be successful or happy."

"Change your thoughts, and you change your world."

"When you get up in the morning, you have two choices—either to be happy or to be unhappy. Just choose to be happy."

"What the mind can conceive and believe, and the heart desire, you can achieve."

"Do not be awestruck by other people and try to copy them. Nobody can be you as efficiently as you can."

"People become really quite remarkable when they start thinking that they can do things. When they believe in themselves, they have the first secret of success."

The Power of Positive Thinking was a remarkable game changer for me when I read it, and it remains one of the most sought-after publications. If you have any doubt about the power of thinking positive, remove the doubt by applying positivity. While I make it sound simple, it is not because there is more magnetic power in negativity. Negativity can become epidemic; it can seem to catch on like a mad virus spreading through a family, an organization, or a relationship.

When someone fails or is projecting negative energy, the results are typically negative. An example is when you fail at something and your first reaction is, "I knew that was going to happen." This may have been due to your pessimistic thinking or a negative vision of the failure. You may have had the gut feeling or intuition that something negative was going to happen during an event, and when it does, you are not surprised. You may have prevented the event from going negative. If you worked proactively and used positive energy, perhaps the event would go off the way you envisioned it. Using positive energy and positive vision can lead to success or victory. Every competitor recognizes the power of positivity, and in a business leadership role, you are always competing to win. You cannot win if you do not believe you can. You cannot change or develop if you do not think you can. It takes believing in yourself in a positive manner to create the change you envision.

The Five Principles in Action

When working with Microsoft Latin America, my collaborative partners were two Brazilian leaders, Clarissa and Anita. Both were originally from Rio de Janeiro, and they relocated to Sao Paulo, Brazil, where they were charged with reorganizing and expanding the first services and support organization for the region. While working side by side with them for well over a year, I learned how to become precise in the focus areas we needed to develop. I also gained a different perspective on planning for self-development and continuous practice while remaining positive, especially during times of ambiguity.

Clarissa and Anita were labeled the "Dynamic Duo," because their energy level was consistently high. It seemed that one could read the other's mind, and they were comfortable making decisions for one another. They finished each other's sentences. When we had our first meeting regarding the build out and integration of an existing services organization, Clarissa was adamant about not making any organizational changes until we were precise on two things. The first was the technical skill set needed for the new organization, and the second was her and Anita's development and integration into a US-based organization. "We must be precise with every move," Anita repeated at each meeting. She was a Six Sigma Black Belt meaning she was educated on how to create strategic plans and therefore wanted facts, data, and measurable insight to determine the best things to do. Clarissa supported Anita and said, "No precision, no plan." We dug into measuring, calculating, and forecasting to ensure that moving people into new roles and expanding the services business was the right thing to do. Clarissa said, "Precision before planning is critical, because we are dealing with people's livelihood." Speaking like a true leader, Clarissa was clearly concerned about her people. Organizational change or integration is often done with little focus on precision thinking, which leads to a lot of ambiguity within the ranks.

Once precision targets and decisions were set, the intensive planning started. We created a business analysis of Strengths, Weakness, Opportunities, and Threats (SWOT) and a personal leadership SWOT for Clarissa and Anita. The business planning processes for both took more than three weeks of daily meetings, and the way that they approached their personal development planning was impressive. They needed to think about assimilating into the US business culture, the language barriers, and the influence they might gain or lose working so closely with their US counterparts. From a first-things-first perspective, they planned on developing their English. "We can promote and articulate what we and our teams are doing in our language, but it is now more important to communicate our strategies in English." Off they went each morning to a one-hour class on business English. Personal and professional plans were done, and it was time to execute. Precision and planning were the most intensive and critical elements of the integration, and they were on target as we measured our success every other week. Clarissa ended our final planning session by creating an event to celebrate our success. It was a team-building event in a small town called Santos. She arranged for the entire team to learn the basics of sailing. Each sailboat had a team of eight people, and our trainers talked about precision and patience in sailing, as it was the symbol of our planning sessions.

Clarissa and Anita practiced their English every day and would role play when preparing a presentation for their US counterparts. They wanted to leave a positive impression each time they communicated with their peers and all who wanted to know how their strategy was unfolding. For personal and professional development plans, they held sessions to practice their communication and presentation styles. They were relentless in working the plans and measuring milestones, and they repeatedly told the stakeholders to have the agreed-upon patience for the results of the organizational change to work. The plan called for twelve months of progress for results to move from a negative to a positive state. When some of our leadership team wanted results sooner, the Dynamic Duo referred to the plan and communicated the current state of the business, which indicated positive growth trends.

From a positivity standpoint, Clarissa and Anita were the best. Because they were so confident in their precision planning process and measured their results and tracking trends every two weeks, they were consistently confident and enthusiastic. They energized their teams and our corporate headquarters with ease as they communicated their progress. When things got derailed, they used positive influence to change course as needed. Clarissa and Anita did not know the term "circle the wagons," but this was the approach they used when there was a hint of negativity. Whenever a situation might turn bad, they encircled it, uncovered the issues, and came up with a solution as quickly as possible.

ASK: When have you experienced precision, planning, practice, patience, and positivity? What worked? What could you have done better?

There is another enlightening *P* that can be added to the five principles, and that is partnership. Clarissa and Anita's partnership was and remains tight. They have a strong, bonded relationship and were partners in this integration and the many more that came their way. Clarissa moved on to a vice president role for another tech company, and Anita remained at Microsoft and prospered in a new role in Europe.

In every event when you employ the five principles of precision, planning, practice, patience, and positivity, you will be on the road to a strategic approach.

How to Lead It 2 Win It®

Event 5: The Five Principles: Precision, Planning, Practice, Patience, and Positivity

Summary and Event Log

> Five principles are used in most forms of development and planning. Where can you apply these principles, and how soon?

> Think through the areas you need to develop the most. Use precision thinking for your outcome. List the top three areas.

> Begin tracking your practice sessions on the areas you are developing. Measure how often you practice and the results that practice brings you.

> Does negativity overpower your thinking? If so, what do you need to start, stop, or continue doing to remain consistently positive?

Precision, planning, practice, patience, and positivity can be core in anything you do. Practice the principles a few times, and soon they will be a new habit.

EVENT 6
LEADERSHIP SWOT

"Begin with the end in mind."

STEPHEN COVEY

EVENT 6
LEADERSHIP SWOT

This event reveals how to build on the areas you want to personally develop. By now, your journey in developing your leadership traits and attributes should be in line with your personal development plans. SWOT is the well-known acronym for Strengths, Weakness, Opportunities, and Threats. SWOT analysis is a strategic planning tool commonly used in businesses and organizations when defining objectives for a move-forward strategy on a project or a merger or acquisition. It allows decision makers to weigh positives and negatives and identify areas to address.

The same applies for your leadership development. Every leader should know what his or her strengths are and how to use them to the best advantage. Sometimes your strengths can also be labeled as weaknesses. They can be so hidden that you don't realize you have a weakness until feedback from others calls it out.

When you develop leadership qualities, there are multiple opportunities to seek out and challenge yourself to develop ways to turn your weaknesses into strengths. Some of these weaknesses may be a threat to your career or professional development. Creating a personal leadership SWOT matrix helps you define your comfort level as a leader. SWOT analysis in business is no different from the one for leadership development. You have already begun to measure your personal strengths and weaknesses by way of feedback and comparison to your role model, and you have identified areas to improve. We will examine the threats that may exist for personal development.

As described in event five, there are seven key inspection areas of a business plan or strategy: the business environment, customer needs, the competition, organization needs, cross-functional needs, productivity, and finance/budgets. Once extensive research is done on these areas, a SWOT analysis is conducted to determine the overall strengths, weaknesses, opportunities, and threats for the business to move forward on.

In creating a SWOT analysis for your leadership development, use the same format of research and data mining, but base it on your areas of need. There are six personal inspection areas, some of which we have already examined: Significance of Acceptance/the feedback loop; examining your leadership traits, style, and attributes; your role model Mirror Map; recognizing your Culture Identity; measuring your balance of confidence and communications; and how you use the five principles for managing events.

Let's begin with the four key areas of your personal SWOT.

Strengths in your personal analysis are the attributes you have discovered from assessment measures that are considered important in furthering your personal development. Examples of strengths often cited are being an experienced leader, being a strong communicator, and demonstrating clear values and attributes. Others include maintaining consistency in leadership style or developing people to include diversity and succession planning.

Weaknesses in your personal analysis formula have to do with factors that could hinder your development toward success. Low-confidence, weak communication skills, limited leadership ability, poor results from employee surveys, and a lack of influence are some areas to examine. Without influence, leadership does not exist. Therefore, if influence is shown to be an area of weakness, it is imperative to research and determine ways to turn it around.

Opportunities typically have to do with elements that will prove helpful in achieving your personal goals for development. Factors could be the positive perception you have with your team, peers, or client base. Opportunities can be derived from weaknesses as well as from your strengths. They can come from lessons learned from your role model or peer group and feedback sessions.

Threats are the final and essential component for your personal analysis. These are factors that could threaten the success of your vision and needs; they should be listed and addressed. Among the threats that are critical to any personal analysis are negative perceptions you may have within your organization or the inability to dedicate time or money for continued personal development.

The underlying purpose of a personal SWOT analysis as a leadership development tool is to compile the relevant factors and seek answers to four essential queries. These queries, as conducted in a business SWOT, comprise a process usually referred to as USED. USED is an acronym for four points to explore: Use each strength, Stop each weakness, Exploit each opportunity, and Defend against each threat.

Creating your personal SWOT is when you put your development areas together. My event of using SWOT for my personal development was almost twenty-four years ago when I was part of a Leadership Development Program (LDP) for executives. At that time, I had my first 360 assessment done by my peer group and my direct reports, a staff of eighty-two people. I completed my first Myers-Briggs personality assessment. Combining these assessments to form a smaller version of a SWOT on myself was an eye opener. As I worked with my facilitator for the 360 and Myers-Briggs assessments, I was defensive about what the data said. Jesse, my facilitator, became one of my professional mentors. Based on her assessment of me over a few months, she confirmed the areas needing development. We dug into the data of the 360 and called out positive areas that we classified as strengths: *caring, charismatic, analytical, focused*, and *strategic*. Hearing that these were my areas of strength made me feel good, and I pumped up my chest like a proud father. When we reviewed areas of weakness that I needed to improve, my chest quickly deflated, and my defense mechanisms kicked in. Areas such as *being a micromanager, overconfident, direct*, and *outspoken* were traits I did not realize that I exhibited. I told Jesse that much of this was news to me. She asked me if hearing the areas labeled as strengths was also news, and I said that for the most part they were not. She told me that I could identify with the positive areas but not so much with the negative areas.

As we reviewed the Myers-Briggs assessment, it also called out areas that I thought I was strong in. It labeled me as an introvert, and I was surprised that the assessment did not confirm how extroverted I was or thought I was. Again, Jesse recognized my personal disconnect with some of the data. I took all the feedback personally. Jesse and I went through each area to build my development. We created a plan of opportunities that focused on areas identified as weaknesses or threats to my development. My analysis from those assessments allowed me to recognize the significance of accepting feedback from others you work or live with on a daily basis. With these feedback tools, I was able to understand and create my personal SWOT.

The SWOT analysis is a "balance sheet" that teaches you how to build each area to ensure that you are set up to succeed. A good personal SWOT analysis should give you clear, succinct, organized information and insights that help you think strategically and make decisions about the future.

The Johari Window

When I help people develop their personal SWOT, I want to make sure that they understand four other dimensions of how the feedback is interpreted. As I mentioned earlier, when I received feedback through a 360 and self-assessment, I was surprised by some of the details. When Jesse asked if some of the information was news to me, we had a deep discussion on how to prevent future surprises, and this led to having open and honest discussions with peers and direct reports. Years later, while attending a sales seminar, I was introduced to the "nowhere to hide" thought process that comes from the Johari Window, and I became aware of how others viewed me. Through this window, you learn how you assimilate information about yourself. It also demonstrates how you may be perceived by others.

The Johari Window was created by Joseph Luft and Harry Ingham in 1955, and it is used to help people better understand their relationships with themselves and others. It is used primarily in self-help groups and corporate settings as a heuristic exercise. I use it during individual and team assessment processes, because the concept is related to the ideas propounded in the Myers-Briggs Type Indicator. For this practice, the reality check is on the feedback and assessments and your understanding of your traits and attributes. The Johari "house" has four windows:

Arena window: *(Known to Self, Known to Others)* is the part of ourselves that we see *and* others see. This is our open book, noticeable to all. Typically these are the open communications that we share.

Blind Spot window: *(Not Known to Self, Known to Others)* is the aspect(s) that others see but we are not aware of. Feedback or 360 assessments typically bring this out. This is what we intentionally think we conceal from others.

Unknown window: *(Not Known to Self, Not Known to Others)* is the most mysterious aspect. This subconscious part of us is not seen by ourselves or others. In the communication process, sometimes our body language tells a story different from what we say. We may not be aware of this, but others can see or read it.

Façade window: *(Known to Self, Not Known to Others)* is our private space that we know but keep from others. If you are insecure or lack confidence on an issue, no one will know. You are aware of it but may put on a facade.

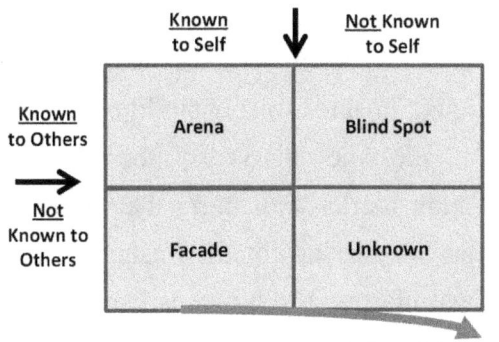

No Place To Hide

When you examine these windows, validating how you perceive yourself versus how others see you should become clear. In essence there is "no place to hide," as you explore each of the windows in depth. Understanding these windows should complement the feedback you have received and is another significant eye opener in how you communicate or behave.

During my first self-assessments, the news was my Blind Spot window. It was known to others that I was presenting traits of being a micromanager, overconfident, direct, and outspoken. As Jesse and I dug in deeper into the data, we found areas that were known to me but not known to others. These were my feelings of insecurity and shyness. While I projected being secure and outgoing, I was in fact, putting on a facade.

ASK: Applying what you have just learned about the Johari window, have you ever been surprised by Window 3, the Unknown (Not Known to Self, Not Known to Others)? How did you respond when you were told of a behavior that you exhibited, but were not aware of?

Another example of moving from one window to another comes from one of my direct reports at Microsoft. He was extremely passionate about his team and his area of business responsibility. He was a director with a large organization, and when his yearly 360 assessments were conducted, he received high marks, indicating that he was a people-focused manager and that his passion for the business mapped to the way he operated. What was alarming to him was that he operated with a lot of insecurities, which made him a bit nervous. He understood his business well and put the right effort into developing his people, but he put on a facade and hid how insecure he felt as a leader of such a large organization. This was known to him but not to others, and he hid his insecurities well. A 360 assessment would not indicate how insecure he was, so he kept doing what he was doing, but the insecurities brought additional stress to his position. He conducted a personality type assessment similar to Myers-Briggs, and it validated what he knew. The personality assessment was part of group training, so he exposed what he was hiding to his team.

Some of his team members were unaware of his insecurity, and some suspected it. After the assessment was done, the window shifted from Facade to Arena. What was known to him was now known to others, and this relieved him from hiding his insecurities, thus relieving the stress he was putting on himself. I created a leadership SWOT for him at the same time, allowing him to see his insecurities as an opportunity to develop.

Writing Your Personal SWOT

Be coldly analytical in developing your personal SWOT. You can't let ego or "selective perception" color your thinking to the extent that you do not see things as they are. Do not overestimate your strengths and opportunities or underestimate your weaknesses and threats. This should help you achieve the following:

- Fully exploit future opportunities for your self-development.

- Combat and overcome competencies, feedback, problems, and threats.

- Anchor your strategic development to build leadership qualities, traits, disciplines, and/or behavioral strengths.

Knowing your real strengths and capabilities, whether they are people, technical, processes, or personal brand, helps you determine what to leverage or build on. Identifying your weaknesses and threats reveals the real limitations and barriers that stand in the way of achieving what you need to in the future.

SWOT is a method of organizing your facts, interpreting them, and summarizing them to determine your real competencies and opportunities. Out of all the feedback, assessments, theories, and attributes you have gathered, what are your major or most important strengths, weaknesses, opportunities, and threats?

Note that not all feedback or assessments are of equal significance. Your personal SWOT analysis is the tool you use to separate the critical from the relevant yet "nice to know" information. Your personal SWOT analysis should not be a new fact- or trend-gathering stage. You may find news here, but it may be news to only you, not to others. Follow the learning from the Johari Window to help you monitor your information.

By understanding and bringing together elements of the Core Events of Leadership, you can create the first element of your personal SWOT.

Think through your lessons learned and self-assessment from the following:

- Understanding the use and value of personal or professional feedback

- Gaining 360 or professional assessments

- The theories and attributes and where your leadership abilities apply

- Understanding the significance of role modeling and the gap between you and the person

- Leveraging the thought leadership behind the JOHARI Window

Are you a confident communicator?

What did you learn from the five principles?

What are the opportunities and learning from culture identity

Think through your SWOT analysis, and list the top three to five areas in each box. With your SWOT, you will be able to create your personal development plan by filling in what you have discovered about yourself. Reflect on the following questions:

- What does the assessment tell you?

- What leadership versus management traits do you exhibit?

- What style/type of leader are you?

    o What type do you think you are?

- What attributes do you need to develop?

  o Courage, wisdom, value driven, serenity?

- Are you a role model now?

  o At home? At work? With your peers? Friends or team?

Understand each of the quadrants. When completing your personal SWOT, think through the areas as outlined, and use the Johari Window as a tool to record a thorough balance sheet.

Strengths	Weaknesses
What you do best!	Just the opposite—the restrictions or deficiencies that limit your accomplishment.
Opportunities	Threats
Typically, external circumstances, events, or situations that offer you good chances to achieve or exceed your objectives.	Opposite of opportunities—the external forces, factors, or events that might create problems or endanger your ability to achieve objectives.

As you review the events, continue to add to your personal leadership SWOT. Think through the most critical areas that you need to develop. Knowing your real strengths and capabilities helps you determine what to leverage or build on. Based on comparisons with your role models, your communication skills, and your culture identity, you should have a clear, succinct, and organized leadership SWOT.

How to Lead It 2 Win It®

Event 6: Leadership SWOT

Summary and Event Log

Create your Leadership SWOT

Process your thinking using the six areas of inspection: 1) Significance of Acceptance/the feedback loop, 2) examining your leadership traits, style, and attributes, 3) your role model Mirror Map, 4) recognizing your culture identity, 5) measuring your balance of confidence and communications, and 6) how you use the five principles for managing events.

Strengths	Weaknesses

Opportunities	Threats

EVENT 7
LEADERSHIP TO STEWARDSHIP

"To be yourself in a world that is constantly trying to make you something else is the greatest accomplishment."

RALPH WALDO EMERSON

EVENT 7
LEADERSHIP TO STEWARDSHIP

This final event is about how to recognize the privilege of leadership and how to consistently remain a steward to yourself, your family, your business, and those you lead. By now, your journey in developing your leadership traits should be in line with your personal development plan. Using a clear definition of leadership and your discovery of your strengths through the core events, you can now define yourself as a steward of a business, team, organization, or family. You are in the place you are in to serve and to steward those around you.

Anthony Robbins writes the following: "The spirit of great leadership is the capacity to take visions and to influence others to do more than they would ever have done on their own. Great leaders help people raise their own standards so that regardless of whether or not the leader is present, the organization or individual still performs at a higher level than ever before. At its essence, leadership is the ability to inspire people. It's the ability to ignite the human spirit and execute consistently." (Robbins, 1986)

Leadership guru Peter Block, author of *Stewardship: Choosing Service over Self-Interest*, suggests the following: "Stewardship is our best response to our search for better leaders. It finally acknowledges the fact that we are all in this together. Leadership as we know it tries to answer the question 'What's in it for me?' Wrong question! The only question that matters is 'What do we want to create together?' This is the most compelling question we can ask in business today." (Block, 2013)

Becoming a steward of a community, organization, business, or family means that you have a common understanding and ownership. It implies a unified ownership with shared accountabilities. Peter Block further describes stewardship as the choice to preside over the orderly distribution of power. He writes, "Stewardship is giving people at the bottom and the boundaries of the organization choice over how to serve a customer, a citizen or a community. It is the willingness to be accountable for the well-being of the larger organization by operating in service, rather than in control, of those around us. Stated simply, it is accountability without control or compliance." (Block, 2013)

The term "stewardship" is commonly used in religion, as in the Bible, which indicates that stewardship is the inherent standard to those whom God calls leaders. Biblical verses on stewardship can be found at Psalm 24:1, Proverbs 3:9–10, Romans 12:6, 1 Corinthians 4:1–2 and 6:19–20, 2 Corinthians chapters 8–9, Ephesians 5:15–16, and James 1:17. Overall, the biblical perspective of stewardship is defined as utilizing and managing all resources God provides for the glory of God and the betterment of his creation. A steward does not own anything—he or she is to make their master a profit. Stewards are to be trustworthy. Deuteronomy 8:17–18 reads as follows: "You may say to yourself, my power and the strength of my hands have produced this wealth for me. But remember the LORD your God, for it is he who gives you the ability to produce wealth, and so confirms his covenant, which he swore to your forefathers, as it is today."

Stewardship in the biblical sense is managing everything God brings into the believer's life in a manner that honors God and impacts eternity. Church ministers, pastors, priests, and rabbis are all labeled as stewards for all those who follow the beliefs in God. From a Christian perspective, the fundamental principle of stewardship is that we own nothing, and God owns everything. We are called upon as managers or stewards of what he has given us.

Stewardship brings on the responsibility of "generational transfer." I first heard this term when I heard James Peacocke, author of *Doing Business God's Way,* speak at an event in Dallas. His concept of generational transfer involves the transfer and obligation of family wealth. In the move from leadership to stewardship, I use this to imply the need to share your learning, transfer the knowledge to mentor, teach, coach, consult, and give back. Stewardship is the obligation to share what you know, what you have learned, and what you have experienced with everyone you work with or meet and those in need of your knowledge. Generational transfer is your obligation to give back so that others can have it easier than you may have had.

In *The 7 Habits of Highly Effective People*, Covey takes readers through a journey of powerful lessons of change, moving from dependence to independence and then interdependence. In the seventh habit, he describes the concept of "sharpening the saw." While Covey does not use the term stewardship, the seventh habit reveals an enlightening passage of renewing the four dimensions of your nature: physical, spiritual, mental, and social/emotional. These dimensions resonated with me. It was a clear message to first become stewards of ourselves, so we can lead and steward others. As Covey describes, the physical involves caring for you through nutrition and exercise. The spiritual dimension is your faith and ability to reflect through meditation as it fits to your core values. The mental dimension involves continuous improvement and expanding your mind through reading, writing, and training of your thought processes. The social/emotional dimension comes from the synergy of living and working with others. Stewardship involves these four dimensions, making you a caretaker of your own well-being and the well-being of others.

In Merriam-Webster's dictionary, stewardship is defined as "office duties, obligation, supervising, or managing of something entrusted to one's care." In Wikipedia, stewardship is "an ethic that embodies the responsible planning and management of resources." The concept of stewardship can be applied to the environment, economics, health, property, information, religion, and so on. Stewardship is often linked to the principles of sustainability. The bottom line is that stewardship is about trust; without it, as in leadership, nothing will be accomplished.

The brilliance of leadership to stewardship is that each definition is about the journey you take and the responsibility you own. From the perspective of your findings in *The Core Events of Leadership* to the famous writings from Anthony Robbins, John Maxwell, Stephen Covey, Peter Block, and the Bible, we are all meant to be stewards of ourselves first and then stewards for our communities, organizations, and families.

The Stewardship Journey

At the beginning of this book, I made it clear that there are thousands of books on the interpretation of leadership, as it comes in many forms. However, "stewardship" brings on a more consistent interpretation, because it calls for full accountability of yourself and your obligation to others, your faith, world, community, family, environment, and the people you associate with.

In this self-improvement and leadership context, I repeat Peter Block's definition of stewardship as "the willingness to be held accountable for the well-being of the larger organization by operating in service, rather than control, of those around us." On the journey, you lead by being a steward to all those you deal with at home, at work, and at your place of worship. You create a collaborative community composed of all who are stewards of shared responsibilities. When you are given the privilege of leading others, the responsibility is to maintain an open relationship and to move forward on your organization's shared vision and mission.

The time you put into the company you are employed by is rented time, and you have the responsibility to care for it as if it were your own. You take care of the business more because it is not yours; you are a steward who has partial responsibility for the overall business. If you are an entrepreneur and an independent businessman or businesswoman, your stewardship is solely owned, but you become the steward of the services or product that you promote. If you are a college student using government funds or loans to pay for your education or are using money from your family, your obligation is to fulfill and steward the expected results. All are recognized not for their leadership or meeting their obligations but for stewarding what was loaned to them.

In an organization, the most valuable players are typically those who go unrecognized. They are those of the front-line organization, and recognizing them is the most precious commodity leaders can bestow. They are the ones who know what the client really needs. Front-line teams are the true stewards of the organization, and stewardship should not stop at the next level or the one next to that. However, it always seems to stop when managers feel compelled to exercise their right to be a top-down leader rather than a collaborative steward of the business.

The journey you have taken through Significance of Acceptance, the Art of Role Modeling, Culture Identity, Confident Communicator, Five Principles, Leadership SWOT, and your road from Leadership to Stewardship brings you to the road of consistency and ownership. As there are multiple events on the journey to leadership, your journey to stewardship will take a deep, methodical view of how to get things done. You will no longer need to ask whether or not you are doing the right things.

With stewardship, doing the right thing will be natural!

How to Lead It 2 Win It®

Event 7: Leadership to Stewardship

Summary and Event Log

Stewardship is the art of leading naturally and becoming interdependent and collaborative in all you do!

Have you seen those who fully understand the concepts of stewardship? What are their behaviors? What sets them apart?

What skills or attributes do you have that will allow you to become a steward of your business, community, or family?

What is your interpretation of stewardship?

List the top five things you need to do to become a steward in your business.

1.

2.

3.

4.

5.

CONCLUSION

Through your leadership journey, you will experience events that trigger a variety of leadership opportunities. You will make different kinds of decisions throughout your professional life. You will attend functions, meetings, and presentations, and you will take on different roles in leading others. Whether you lead a large team or a small one, you will be judged on your performance —not just by those who work for you but by all those who work with you. Leadership is a privilege and, as mentioned, all are watching you.

As you practice and develop your skills, keep the following in mind:

- A leadership event is recognized as an important incident that locks into your memory.

- True leaders know the importance of feedback! Recognize the power of the feedback, and take the right course of action to change.

- Know that the only thing stopping you from becoming who you want to be is you!

- Role modeling takes practice, practice, and more perfect practice.

- Understand your work culture, and create an environment or listening system that ensures that the voice of the organizational culture is heard; this can make or break a company.

- Effective communication is the strongest asset a leader can bring to demonstrate, motivate, and inspire confidence.

- Precision, planning, practice, patience, and positivity can become core in anything you do.

- Learn to use a leadership SWOT analysis to move forward from leadership to stewardship.

The Core Events of Leadership is designed for aspiring managers, tenured leaders, and individual contributors. From each of these organizational levels, the feedback I have received when using this book as the foundation of training has been extremely positive. I can now only hope and wish you a rewarding and successful journey from leadership to stewardship.

BIBLIOGRAPHY

Block, Peter. *Stewardship: Choosing Service over Self-Interest*. San Francisco: Berrett-Koehler Publishers, 2013.

Cameron, Kim, and Robert Quinn. *Diagnosing and Changing Organizational Culture: Based on the Competing Values Framework.* San Francisco: Jossey-Bass, 2011.

Charan, Ram. *Leadership in the Era of Economic Uncertainty.* New York: McGraw-Hill, 2009.

Conner, Daryl R. *Leading at the Edge of Chaos.* Danvers, MA: John Wiley & Sons, 1998.

Covey, Stephen. *The 7 Habits of Highly Effective People.* New York: Free Press, 2004.

Drucker, Peter, and Ken Blanchard. *The One Minute Manager.* New York: William Morrow Company, 1982.

Gladwell, Malcolm. *Outliers.* New York: Little, Brown and Company, 2008.

Kotter, John P., and James L. Heskett. *Corporate Culture and Performance.* New York: Simon & Schuster, 1992.

Lencioni, Patrick. *The Five Dysfunctions of a Team.* San Francisco: Jossey-Bass, 2002.

Levinson, Jay Conrad, and Andrew Neitlich. *Guerrilla Marketing for a Bulletproof Career.* Garden City, NY: Morgan James, 2010.

Maxwell, John C. *The 21 Irrefutable Laws of Leadership.* Nashville, TN: Thomas Nelson, 2007.

Neitlich, Andrew. *How to Coach Executives.* Charleston, SC: ATN Associates, 2012.

Nichols, Lisa. *Chicken Soup for the African American Woman's Soul.* Deerfield Beach, FL: Health Communications, 2006.

Peal, Norman Vincent. *The Power of Positive Thinking.* New York, NY: Ishi Press, 2011.

Peacocke, James. *Doing Business God's Way.* Santa Rosa, CA: REBUILD, 2003.

Robbins, Anthony. *Awaken the Giant Within.* New York: Free Press, 1991.

Robbins, Anthony. *Unlimited Power.* New York: Free Press, 1986.

Thielen, David. *The 12 Simple Secrets of Microsoft Management.* New York: McGraw-Hill, 1999.

Tylor, Edward B. *Primitive Culture.* Cambridge, New York: Cambridge University Press, 2012.

Walton, Mary. *The Deming Management Method: 14 Points for Management.* Foreword by W. Edwards Deming. New York: Berkley Publishing, 1986.

Carlos A Merla

"Leadership is an event that brings notable attention worth repeating."

CARLOS MERLA *is a Master Certified Coach Trainer (MCCT) and accredited Certified Executive Coach (CEC). An author and a trainer, he has more than thirty years of experience in the corporate world developing sales organizations at PM/Altria Group. He spent the last fifteen years as international services director for Microsoft Corporation. He is known for his extensive international business experience in Latin America and Southeast Asia, which allows him to speak and deliver leadership workshops worldwide.*

Contact: Carlos@Merlaleadership.com

Website: merlaleadership.com